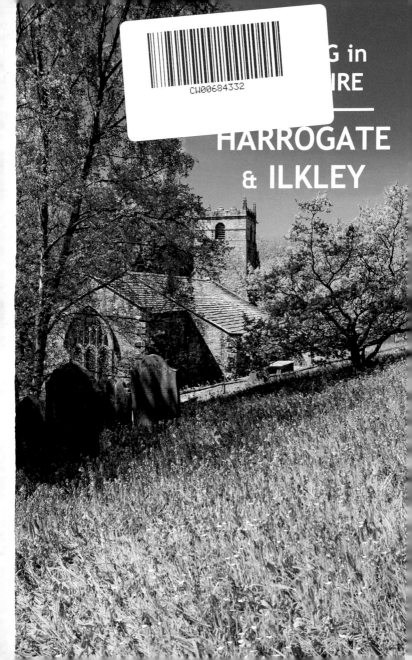

G in
IRE

HARROGATE
& ILKLEY

CW00684332

HILLSIDE GUIDES - ACROSS THE NORTH

Yorkshire River Photobooks
•JOURNEY OF THE WHARFE

Easy Walks •50 YORKSHIRE WALKS FOR ALL

Walking in Yorkshire - North/East (25 Walks)
•NORTH YORK MOORS South/West   •NORTH YORK MOORS North/East
•YORKSHIRE WOLDS   •HOWARDIAN HILLS & VALE OF YORK

Walking in Yorkshire - West/South/Mid (25 Walks)
•AIRE VALLEY & BRONTE COUNTRY   •HARROGATE & ILKLEY
•CALDERDALE & SOUTH PENNINES   •SOUTH YORKSHIRE

Walking in Yorkshire - Yorkshire Dales (25 Walks)
•East: NIDDERDALE & RIPON   •West: THREE PEAKS & HOWGILL FELLS
•South: WHARFEDALE & MALHAM •North: WENSLEYDALE & SWALEDALE

Circular Walks - Lancashire/North West/North Pennines
•BOWLAND   •PENDLE & RIBBLE   •ARNSIDE & SILVERDALE
•LUNESDALE   •EDEN VALLEY   •ALSTON & ALLENDALE

Long Distance Walks
•COAST TO COAST WALK   •DALES WAY   •CUMBRIA WAY
•PENDLE WAY   •CALDERDALE WAY

Hillwalking - Lake District (25 Walks)
•LAKELAND FELLS - SOUTH   •LAKELAND FELLS - EAST
•LAKELAND FELLS - NORTH   •LAKELAND FELLS - WEST

Short Scenic Walks (30 Walks)
•NORTH YORK MOORS   •HARROGATE & NIDDERDALE

Short Scenic Walks (20 Walks)
•UPPER WHARFEDALE •INGLETON/WESTERN DALES •RIBBLESDALE
•MALHAMDALE   •SWALEDALE   •SEDBERGH/DENTDALE
•UPPER WENSLEYDALE •LOWER WENSLEYDALE
•ILKLEY/WASHBURN VALLEY •AIRE VALLEY •HAWORTH
•HEBDEN BRIDGE •AROUND PENDLE •RIBBLE VALLEY •BOWLAND

*Send for a detailed current catalogue and price list
and also visit www.hillsidepublications.co.uk*

WALKING in YORKSHIRE

———

HARROGATE & ILKLEY

Paul Hannon

———

Hillside

HILLSIDE PUBLICATIONS

2 New School Lane
Cullingworth
Bradford
West Yorkshire
BD13 5DA

First published 2019

© Paul Hannon 2019   ISBN 978-1-907626-16-6

Cover illustrations: Cow & Calf Rocks; Knaresborough
Back cover: Washburn Valley; Page One: Fewston; Page Three: Red kite
Above: River Washburn; Opposite: White Wells, Ilkley Moor
(Paul Hannon/Yorkshire Photo Library)

The sketch maps are based on 1947 Ordnance Survey One-Inch maps

Printed in China on behalf of Latitude Press

CONTENTS

INTRODUCTION

The affluent former spa towns of Harrogate and Ilkley lie at the heart of archetypal Yorkshire countryside, amid abundant walking opportunities ranging from rolling moorland to pastoral riverbanks. Ilkley stands on the River Wharfe, fresh from leaving the Yorkshire Dales to enjoy a more sedate journey through the Wharfe Valley to Wetherby. Harrogate sits above another Dales river, the Nidd, centrepiece to its vibrant neighbour Knaresborough. In between Wharfe and Nidd, the River Washburn occupies its own characterful valley, joining the Wharfe near Otley.

Ilkley is best known for the celebrated Ilkley Moor, a bracing tract of heather upland that thrusts itself boldly above the town, and once upon its open heath you could be many miles from the busy streets below. Gritstone edges and crags occur all over the moor, the major outcrops being around the famous Cow & Calf Rocks. The moor itself exhibits rich evidence of early man, being liberally dotted with stone circles, burial cairns and the cup and ring markings that decorate many a dark boulder. In reality, Ilkley Moor is but one part of the great sweep of Rombalds Moor, a mighty upland ridge forming a high southern boundary to this area. A lower continuation of this ridge is formed by Otley Chevin, a popular tract of country guarding its little town below.

The summit of Rombalds Moor reaches 1319ft/402m above sea level, but its northern counterpart across the Wharfe manages to oust it as the highest point in the book. Here, Round Hill overlooks a lonelier reach of expansive moorland high above rural communities such as Langbar and Denton. These quietly farmed lower slopes are interspersed with parkland belonging to great houses of centuries past. Into the 21st century the houses remain, echoes of an age largely consigned to the history books.

The Washburn Valley, which again starts out on high moors, is another contrasting area, featuring timewarp settlements such as Timble and Fewston. The Washburn's winding miles are dominated by a chain of reservoirs harnessing the river in a manner that has largely blended into the scene: now viewed as an integral feature, they are cushioned by densely wooded slopes that make their own valued contribution. Indeed, the Washburn Valley sits within the Nidderdale Area of Outstanding Natural Beauty.

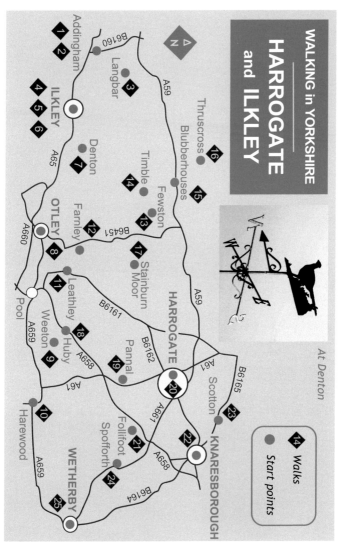

WALKING in YORKSHIRE

HARROGATE
and ILKLEY

At Denton

◆ 14 Walks

● Start points

INTRODUCTION

The eastern half of this region is based on the floral town of Harrogate and its hugely colourful partner Knaresborough. This tract of countryside is a rich tapestry of patchwork fields, cosy stone villages and stately old houses and parkland. It is also littered with a surprising array of features, from landmark rock outcrops to ancient earthworks. You will discover Roman roads, old railway lines, historic paths and trackways; colourful woodland and elegant parks; inspiring churches and hunting lodges; Victorian spas and ancient farmsteads.

Norman castles are in evidence at Knaresborough, Spofforth and Harewood – an intriguing contrast with the stately splendour of Harewood House itself. Idyllic villages like Follifoot and Kirkby Overblow are found in amongst natural wonders such as Almscliff Crag, Spofforth Pinnacles and Plumpton Rocks. Both the Nidd and Wharfe rivers offer delightful footpaths along tranquil stretches shared only with the odd angler, and although they generally flow wide and calm in these sedate lower reaches, the Nidd Gorge near Knaresborough proves an exception.

It is a positive prospect that the towns of Harrogate, Ilkley, Otley, Wetherby and Knaresborough are all capable of offering a splendid walk starting in their very heart. A great success of recent years has been the release of Red kites on the Harewood estate, and today these graceful specimens might be spotted soaring almost anywhere in this skies above you – indeed this book could be subtitled 'Walks in Red Kite country', such is their profusion.

Access to the countryside

The majority of walks are on public rights of way with no access restrictions, or long-established access areas and permissive paths. A handful also take advantage of Right to Roam: any walks making use of Open Country are noted in their introduction, though on most days of the year you are free to walk responsibly over these wonderful landscapes. Of the restrictions that do pertain, the two most notable are that dogs are normally banned from grouse moors (other than on rights of way); and that the areas can be closed to walkers for up to 28 days each year, subject to advance notice. The most likely times will be from the 'Glorious Twelfth', the start of the grouse shooting season in August, though weekends should largely be unaffected. Further information can be obtained from

Natural England, and ideally from information centres. Finally, bear in mind that in spring, avoiding tramping over open country away from paths helps safeguard vulnerable ground-nesting birds.

Although bus services within the area are generally limited, availability, if any, is mentioned in the introduction to each walk. There are railway stations at Harrogate, Knaresborough, Pannal, Weeton, Ilkley, Ben Rhydding and Burley-in-Wharfedale.

Using the guide

The walks range from 4$\frac{1}{2}$ to 9 miles, with the average distance being around 6$\frac{1}{2}$ miles. Each walk is self-contained, with essential information being followed by a concise route description and a simple map. Dovetailed in between are snippets of information on features along the way: these are placed in *italics* to ensure that the all important route description is easier to locate. Start point postcodes are a rough guide only for those with 'satnav': grid references are more precise!

The sketch maps serve to identify the location of the routes rather than the fine detail, and whilst the description should be sufficient to guide you around, the appropriate Ordnance Survey map is recommended. To gain the most from a walk, the detail of a 1:25,000 scale Explorer map is unsurpassed. It also gives the option to vary walks as desired, giving a much improved picture of your surroundings and the availability of any linking paths for shortening or lengthening walks. Just two maps cover all the walks:

• *Explorer 289 - Leeds*
• *Explorer 297 - Lower Wharfedale & Washburn Valley*

Also very useful for planning is Landranger map 104.

Useful contacts

Information Centres

Royal Baths, Crescent Road **Harrogate** HG1 2RR • 01423-537300
Town Hall, Station Road **Ilkley** LS29 6HB • 01943-602319
Nelson Street **Otley** LS21 1EZ • 01943-462485
17 Westgate **Wetherby** LS22 6LL • 01937-582151
Castle Courtyard, Market Place **Knaresborough** HG5 8AE • 01423-866886
Nidderdale AONB The Old Workhouse, King Street, Pateley Bridge HG3 5LE (01423-712950)   www.nidderdaleaonb.org.uk
Open Access • 0845-100 3298   www.countrysideaccess.gov.uk

WINDGATE NICK

An exhilarating march along the 'Wharfedale edge' with beautiful views, sandwiched between delectable pastures

START *Addingham (SE 078497; LS29 0LY)*

DISTANCE *7^{1}4 miles (11^{1}2km)*

ORDNANCE SURVEY 1:25,000 MAP
Explorer 297 - Lower Wharfedale & Washburn Valley

ACCESS *Start at foot of Main Street, in vicinity of Fleece pub. Memorial Hall car park. Keighley-Ilkley and Skipton-Ilkley bus.*

The street village of Addingham was the scene in 1826 of a thousand-strong Luddite riot, an abortive attempt to break into the mill to smash power looms. Today, little industry remains in what was the first major mill settlement on the Wharfe. Despite its 1991 by-pass, Addingham's main street retains much bustle, and supports five pubs, tearooms and several shops. Descend Main Street towards Ilkley, and near the foot of the village go left on Church Street to a junction with North Street. Virtually opposite, to your left, a short way runs between houses to a small stone-arched bridge on Town Beck into the grounds of the church. *Parts of St Peter's date from medieval times, while the nave sports a fine oak roof. A small Saxon cross is preserved showing two figures under a cross. Seek also the mouse carvings of the famous Kilburn workshops.* Bear right on a grassy path off the surfaced path, crossing the grassy sward beneath the church to a stone-arched footbridge on Town Beck. Across it, a few steps lead up onto Low Mill Lane. Turn left past the imposing old rectory set in delightful grounds.

At the road's demise alongside the River Wharfe you enter Low Mill Village, a tasteful 1980s development of this old mill corner. *Just across the weir on the river, Castleberg Scar is an Iron Age dwelling site.* Keep straight on the access road out of the other end to a T-junction with the old Ilkley road. Turn left to run parallel with the Wharfe. At the first opportunity take a gate on the left sending a path along a riverside pasture. At the end a gate sends the path up a wooded

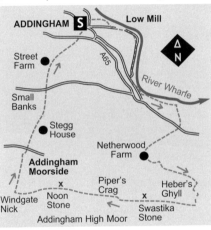

bank: at the top, ignore a footbridge in front and leave the river's environs by turning right up an enclosed path at The Hollins. This rises pleasantly between hedgerows to emerge onto a drive just short of the A65. *To the right is a turnpike milestone, while at this point the old Ilkley-Skipton railway crossed the road.*

Go left a few yards on the footway and cross to a stile opposite. Go briefly right along the fieldside, soon deflected left by a fence to a corner gate. Through it go left with the fence, soon veering right across the field to find a stile behind a streamlet in the top corner. Advance briefly with the fence on your left to another stile, through which angle gently right up this large sloping field. A reedy streamlet leads up to an old gateway at the top right. Resume along the field top to a stile, and continue on to a kissing-gate onto a driveway. From a stile opposite rise left to the house at Netherwood Farm, once a cluster of farmsteads.

A small gate puts you outside the house, where go left on the drive the short way to a junction. Go straight across to the start of an enclosed track, but immediately take a gate on the left into a field. Head away, slanting gently right through a line of trees to rise to a stile in a wall. Continue slanting up towards the houses at Briery Wood Farm to locate a small gate in the top corner. Ascend a wallside to another just above, then rise slightly left to a wall-stile at an old gateway. A hollowed path drops down to the rear of the buildings and along the drive heading out. This quickly meets the end of Heber's Ghyll Drive at a gateway. Here take a small gateway to the right to follow an excellent parallel path along the base of Bracken Wood, profuse with springtime bluebells. This runs to a footbridge at the foot of Heber's Ghyll alongside a former WC.

Don't cross, but take the well-surfaced path rising alongside Heber's Ghyll. The tumbling beck is re-crossed no less than six times during this steep woodland ascent, before arriving at a stone shelter. The right-hand path runs a few strides to a small iron gate onto the foot of Heber Moss, part of all-embracing Rombalds Moor. Go right on the wallside path, through a small gate above the wood corner. Visible ahead are the iron railings guarding the Swastika Stone on Woodhouse Crag. The little path crosses a streamlet and slants left the short way up through bilberry bushes. Keep left at an early fork to quickly emerge on a broader path running right the short way to the Swastika Stone. *Thought to date from the Bronze Age it resembles versions found in Scandinavia: the original is the less obvious carving on the main rock, that at the front being a replica for ease of viewing.*

The path now sets off on a well-defined course across the moor, rising ever gradually through several stiles to reach a cluster of windswept larch trees. Passing through a crumbling wall beyond them, a better-defined edge soon re-forms on Piper's Crag. *Some of the more prominent boulders to your right bear cup & ring markings: abundant on these moors, they are further relics of Bronze Age times. This moor-edge route is part of a prehistoric trade-route, possibly a major link between Ireland and the Continent. It was christened Rombalds Way by a local historian more than half a century ago.*

A string of small metal gates in intervening walls punctuate this classic march beneath Addingham High Moor. *Super views look over Addingham and Bolton Abbey to hazy heights up Wharfedale.* Not long after the distinctive block of the isolated Noon Stone, the final gate sees the path enjoy a short spell in heather away from the edge. *Here is a brief opportunity to survey two major valleys, as Airedale appears over to the left. The Bronte moors rise beyond Keighley and the Worth Valley, while further west you can see as far as the moors of Bowland.* Soon a cairn is reached signalling a path crossroads at Windgate Nick.

Here, yards short of the edge's highest point, descend through the aptly-named Nick into a former quarry. The main path bears right below the cliffs, through a rash of stones and down a grassy groove to a ladder-stile in the wall. A grassy path descends the reedy pasture below, and across a moist area the path drops to a stile in the bottom corner. A wall then leads down through gorse bushes to a stile onto Moorside Lane serving the scattered farms of Addingham Moorside. Cross straight over and down a driveway: as it crosses a beck go left on a short way emerging via a gate/stile into a field. Drop straight down a little bank, bearing left to reach a kissing-gate. Swing left around the scrubby bank below, and drop down outside a small wood to a corner stile/gate. Head away left to a corner stile, and with a chalet park on your left cross to a stile ahead. From this a grassy path bears right down a gorse-draped pasture to a stone-slab footbridge in the bottom corner.

Follow the wall rising left from it, and cross the field centre to a small gate in front of the nearest house at Small Banks. The path runs along a garden edge to a small gate onto a road, Cocking Lane. Just yards to the left, a stile on the right resumes the descent down a fieldside. From a stile at the bottom bear left to one at the wall-end above a wooded bank. A descent of the Cat Steps to a hollow leads to a gate up the other side. *Around this point you cross the line of the Roman road from Ilkley through the Aire Gap to Ribchester: just along to the left, Street Farm's name maintains the link.* Over the little brow bear right down the field, merging with a fence on your right to drop to a gate in the bottom corner. This accesses a stone bridge across the in-filled course of the Ilkley-Skipton railway. Across, take a kissing-gate on the left to encounter Addingham by-pass and cross with care. From an identical gate opposite drop to another, then slant left down to a small gate into the cricket club grounds. Pass left around the pitch to emerge onto the road at the foot of the village, and go left the short way back to the start.

CHELKER RESERVOIR

A beautiful riverside leads to high pastures and big views

START *Addingham (SE 078497; LS29 0LY)*

DISTANCE *6 miles (9$\frac{1}{2}$km)*

ORDNANCE SURVEY 1:25,000 MAP
Explorer 297 - Lower Wharfedale & Washburn Valley

ACCESS *Start at foot of Main Street, in vicinity of Fleece pub.
Memorial Hall car park. Keighley-Ilkley and Skipton-Ilkley bus.*

For a note on Addingham see page 10. From Main Street turn towards Ilkley, and near the foot of the village go left on Church Street to a junction with North Street. Turn left, becoming Bark Lane on a bend before a stepped path turns down to the right. *On the bend stands Ferryman's Cottage, recalling the predecessor of the footbridge you will shortly see.* Quickly forking, the right branch descends to a suspension footbridge over the Wharfe, but your way is the left fork upstream high above the river. Shortly reaching a fork, drop right, closer to the river to run on into an open area at converted High Mill. This deflects you left into a courtyard and straight ahead to a gate into a caravan park. Head away along the drive, but soon after bridging a sidestream, a path returns you to the Wharfe alongside a weir.

The river now leads unfailingly up-dale, a kissing-gate taking you beyond the site into open countryside. After a couple of fields you are temporarily forced up above a steep, wooded bank. From a stile at the top, the path runs on above the trees, and from a stile at the end you drop steeply back to the riverbank at a lovely spot. After further delightful riverbank rambling another wooded bank intervenes beyond a ladder-stile. At the top a stile leads into trees to skirt a house to join the B6160 at Lobwood. Cross to a kissing-gate accessing Farfield Friends' Meeting House. *This splendid Quaker building of 1689 is usually open for peaceful contemplation.* Behind

it turn right on the old Lobwood House drive. Pass through a gate and up to join the drive just above. At this fork take the left one, swinging round into Farfield Livery.

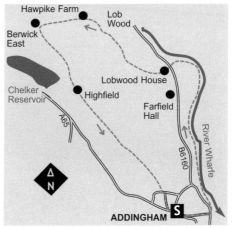

Remain on the firm track rising past stables, and largely enclosed it runs to a rail underpass. *The Skipton-Ilkley line closed in 1965, a sad loss as it linked stations that remain active.* The track runs right to a gate into a field. Slant diagonally up to a redundant gate, and maintain the slant to a wall-stile just above Eller Carr Wood. Now more level, maintain the same line across a large, sloping pasture to a gate/wall-stile above a slightly higher wood top. *The Wharfedale view has opened out, up past Beamsley Beacon, Bolton Bridge, Bolton Abbey and Simon's Seat all the way up to Great Whernside.* Continuing on above the trees, the thin path dips slightly to a gate and tiny stream as Hawpike Farm appears ahead. Cross a small enclosure to a gate onto a track in front of the farm.

Go left away from the buildings, through a gate and right of a modern barn into a field. A broad, grassy way rises steeply away, merging with a grass track rising from the right to reach a gate in the fence above, with a bield (sheep shelter) on your right. Veer

15

slightly right to a gate/stile just ahead, and an improving grassy way runs on below the crest of Haw Pike. With big open views from this turning point of the walk, the way runs invitingly on towards Berwick East Farm. Pass through a gate alongside East Berwick House, then out along its drive. Level with the white-walled farm it swings sharp left to quickly merge with a drive from the right. Leave here on a path bearing left through a pocket of woodland, rising the short way to a fence-stile into a field. Ascend near the wall to a stile in the top corner, with Chelker Reservoir revealed across to your right. Head away with the wall on a broad way along a broad ridge, with the reservoir seen much better now. *This high point of the walk enjoys all-round views, including Rombalds Moor ahead. Along this crest four wind turbines were erected in 1992, one of the country's first multi-mast sites that was dismantled in 2013. The reservoir of 1858 is a favourite haunt of birdlife.*

A stile puts you on the other side of the wall at the end of the field, returning to the right side via the right-hand of two facing gates at a corner recess. Passing the concrete base of what was the last turbine, advance to a gate at the end. Now drop down across a grass track to a wall-stile alongside a small embankment that served an old quarry. Bear left to Highfield Farm, using a gate left of the main buildings to enter the yard. Opposite the house take a gate on the left and cross a field to a gate onto Bracken Ghyll golf course. With a wall across to the right, advance straight on through scattered trees near the edge of the course. A little further a clear path runs through more trees to a stile temporarily off the course. A slender pasture leads on past Highfield House on the right to a stile back onto the course alongside a green. Again continue straight down, passing a stone shed before a clear, inviting path runs through rough grassland and a few trees. Passing a small pond on your right you find a stile at the bottom, leaving the course.

Continue down an inviting wooded avenue. With the ruined barn of High Laithe to your right, the path continues down, parallel with an overgrown sunken way on the left. This remains a lovely course, through a stile and down again to one on the left before the bottom corner. With the now serviceable lane alongside, remain parallel until a kissing-gate at the very bottom gives entry to the lane. This runs on to join a road: go left and turn sharp right on Sugar Hill to re-enter Main Street alongside the old railway.

BEAMSLEY BEACON

A bracing stroll on good paths entirely on open moorland

START *Langbar (SE 093518; LS29 0EU)*

DISTANCE *5$\frac{1}{2}$ miles (8$\frac{3}{4}$km)*

ORDNANCE SURVEY 1:25,000 MAP
Explorer 297 - Lower Wharfedale & Washburn Valley

ACCESS *Start from highest point of Beamsley-Langbar road at Beacon Hill. Modest parking on brow itself, with parking area on open ground on Beamsley side, or at road bend 100 yards east. •OPEN ACCESS - see page 8 (one mile on permissive path).*

From the brow a path heads up open ground between the walls of two gardens. Keep to the path on the left side, slanting left up the moor, through a small reedy patch to then rise pleasantly through heather. Very quickly you reach the foot of a defined ridge, to begin a splendid climb through modest rocks and boulders. When the rocks end, Beamsley Beacon's OS column and cairn appear ahead, and the path continues steadily up to reach them. Just half a mile into the walk and the hard work is over! *At 1289ft/393m the OS column is dwarfed by a huge pile of stones. The column bears a memorial to the Canadian crew (4 killed and 4 survived) of a Lancaster bomber from RAF Leeming that crashed on these slopes in November 1945. The monstrous pile of stones is the remains of a Bronze Age mound, thought to be the burial place of*

17

a local chieftain. Just two centuries ago a beacon was manned here during the Napoleonic wars, and foundations of the beacon guard's house survive.

The largely moorland panorama includes, anti-clockwise from the north-east: Kex Gill Moor, Rocking Moor, Hazlewood Moor, Simon's Seat, Earl Seat, Barden Moor, Flasby Fell, Skipton Moor, Rombalds Moor, Otley Chevin and back to Blubberhouses Moor. Wharfedale occupies the valley floor, though finest feature is the bird's-eye view over the Beamsley and Bolton Bridge area. Appraising the view it becomes apparent there is higher ground five minutes along the ridge, and the path runs to the Old Pike. *At 1312ft/400m its top is marked by a small group of rocks in the heather, this too being the less obvious site of a Bronze Age burial mound.*

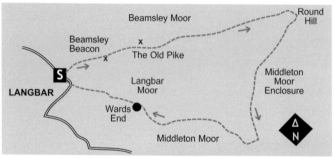

Resume on a well-used continuing permissive path, dropping marginally then running along the flat Beamsley Level between Beamsley Moor and Langbar Moor. The central section can be a little moist, then the path rises gently past the Grey Stone. *This landmark boulder has been utilised as a boundary stone, inscribed BLN referring to the parishes of Beamsley and Nesfield with Langbar.* Beyond it continue rising to reach a standard boundary stone, then on the short way to a sturdy boundary wall ahead at Little Gate. Ignoring gates in it, turn right on the path rising the short way to a gate/stile in a fence/old wall at the crest of Round Hill. *With Otley Chevin and Rombalds Moor to the south the panorama opens out. Northwards, Beamsley Beacon and Barden Moor lead the eye to High Dales country, culminating in Great Whernside's mighty whaleback. Further still, looking west are Lancashire's Pendle Hill*

and Bowland moors. At 1342ft/409m, this is the highest point of the walk. It is also the book's only walk to enter the Yorkshire Dales National Park - though from here-on you are outside it!

Turn right here, with the fence and old wall on your right. This descends some 150 yards to a gate, where it forks. Take the path branching steadily left to commence an excellent, gentle descent of Middleton Moor Enclosure. It remains quite near the wall, and is clear throughout. Initially shadowing a line of reeds, it crosses these to descend close by a line of grouse butts. *March Ghyll Reservoir is seen below.* The path then bears slightly more to the left, passing above a couple of shooting cabins by Loftshaw Gill, then shortly crossing a streamlet and dropping to a gateway in an old fence. Over a heathery knoll it slants down to the last of another line of butts, just beyond which you join a fenceside track on the moor edge. *This is the Badger Gate, once patronised by travelling corn dealers, or 'badgers'.*

Turn right, and crossing Loftshaw Gill the track slants up to a gate in the sturdy descending wall. Through it cross straight over the parallel shooters' track, and take the right-hand of two grassy tracks heading away. This slants gently up above the broad hollow of Delves Slack on Middleton Moor, soon gaining a brow to run very pleasantly along Middle Ridge to a cross-paths marked by an old milestone. *This stumpy stone post faithfully records the miles to Skipton (6), Ot(t)ley (5) and Knar(e)sb(o)rough (11).* Turn right here on the Badger Gate, a thinner path dropping to the wall corner just below, then following the wall beneath Langbar Moor to the rear of the house at Wards End. Its access road leads out for a level stroll across the moor, merging and reaching more houses as it leaves the moor to meet the road junction.

Old guidepost, Middleton Moor

ILKLEY MOOR

A bracing stroll around a wealth of moorland landmarks

START *Ilkley (SE 117471; LS29 9JN)*

DISTANCE *6¹⁄₂ miles (10¹⁄₂km)*

ORDNANCE SURVEY 1:25,000 MAP
Explorer 297 - Lower Wharfedale & Washburn Valley

ACCESS *Start from Darwin Gardens car park immediately above moor-foot cattle-grid at top of Wells Road, which climbs steeply from The Grove. Buses and rail station in town centre.*

Ilkley is the highest town on the River Wharfe, a perfect stepping-stone between industrial conurbations and the Yorkshire Dales. This thriving town blends a workaday existence with that of a tourist venue, its spacious streets decorated by a tapestry of floral colour. All Saints' church has a 500-year old tower, but is best known for its Anglo-Saxon crosses, and also a well-preserved effigy of a 14th century knight, Adam de Middleton. The church covers part of the site of the Roman fort of VERBEIA, built around 79 AD: evidence is restricted to a small section of preserved wall. Also by the church, the splendid 16th century Manor House serves as a community hub, currently open at weekends.

Rejoin the road and cross the cattle-grid on your left, then immediately double back right to rise to a gate set back from a small parking area. Ignore the access road rising left, and take the firm, partly stepped path climbing to the left of a paddling pool. It rises steeply and unfailingly up the moor to reach White Wells. *This humble cottage is a monument to Ilkley's spa days. In the mid-19th century large hydros were built for people to take the therapeutic waters, but a century earlier Squire Middleton built White Wells as a bath-house to enable townsfolk to enjoy a dip in the pure moorland spring water. In the 1970s it was restored and is now a visitor centre serving refreshments and with WCs. Inside is a deep circular pool hollowed from the rock and fed by a cold mineral spring - and still available for a plunge.*

Ilkley flourished as a spa town - the 'Malvern of the North' - and the Victorians revelled in the healing powers of its waters. By the turn of the century the fashion had passed, but by that time Ilkley was firmly on the tourist map. By the time you get here you'll enjoy magnificent views over the town to the bleaker moors opposite, and up the valley into the Dales. Just beneath it to the left is a small tarn. Behind the cottage a stepped path climbs to join a broader one, rising left and running to a fork below a small plantation. Bear right up a stone staircase above the onset of Ilkley Crags. *The lower path runs through Rocky Valley.* Just above the start of the crags the way eases and the real climbing is now complete. The path bears right to a crossroads with a contouring path. Go straight across to advance on up the open moor, now awash with heather. *Dramatic views over Ilkley and the valley are now replaced by wilder moorland.* Quickly arriving at the stream of Backstone Beck, a lesser path comes in from the left.

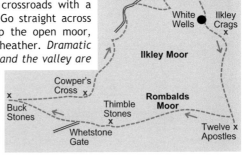

After crossing tiny Backstone Beck here, the path receives an unbroken stone flagged surface, a long level section preceding a short pull towards the prominent boundary stoop of Lanshaw Lad. Only a thin path climbs to it as the main path bears left to suddenly level out, and the flags end. This is the turning point, but the path runs on two minutes further to the Twelve Apostles stone circle. *Presumed to be of Bronze Age origin like so many moorland relics, its dozen stones form a circle some 50 feet in diameter. This well chosen site overlooks both Wharfedale and Airedale, and across to man's more intrusive ornaments on Menwith Hill.* Your onward route retraces steps and turns off along the flagged path running behind Lanshaw Lad. *Inscribed with several sets of initials and the year 1833, Lanshaw Lad marks the division between Ilkley and Burley Moors, and also marks a splendid viewpoint. Landmarks include Barden Moor, Buckden Pike, Great Whernside, Beamsley Beacon, Round Hill, Menwith Hill, Almscliff Crag, the Hambleton Hills on the North York Moors, and Otley Chevin.*

This grand stride runs on for a considerable time set back from the minor edge of White Crag Moss. At a dip it departs the edge and slants left, rising ever gently to reach the Ordnance Survey column on Rombalds Moor summit at 1319ft/402m. *The extensive view offers a host of features across the valley, from Buckden Pike and Great Whernside at the dalehead down to Simon's Seat, Beamsley Beacon, Round Hill, Lippersley Ridge, Menwith Hill, Almscliff Crag and Otley Chevin: westward are Lancashire landmarks Boulsworth Hill and Pendle Hill.* Resume along the flagged path as it angles towards the ridge wall. En route, a few small boulders feature the Puddle Stone. *This 2012 addition to the landscape features the work of poet Simon Armitage, part of his South Pennine Stanza Stones series.* Meeting the Thimble Stones at the wall, the path runs on with the wall to Whetstone Gate (locally known as Keighley Gate). *Through the gate, which is not used, is the fully surfaced terminus of the road climbing from Riddlesden in the Aire Valley. Happily Keighley Road on the Ilkley side has remained unfit for ordinary motors.*

A simple option here is to turn right, omitting the Buck Stones and picking up the full route within five minutes at Cowper's Cross set 50 yards back: a little path breaks off to reach it. The full route crosses straight over and finally encounters 'real' moorland paths, as the intermittently moist wallside path runs to the waiting Buck Stones. Part way on the worst moist section is skirted round to the right, then approaching the nearest massive boulder take the right fork to get there. These are the East Buck Stones, a fine group of boulders. *At 1299ft/396m they mark a focal point of the walk. Apart from excellent views up Wharfedale, they also enjoy a southerly panorama over Airedale.*

A path continues the short way to the watershed wall, where the similarly sited West Buck Stones hover over a pronounced escarpment. *One of these is an inscribed boundary stone, and they offer good shelter from a sudden shower, and similar sweeping views over the moor. Here you can also survey the vastness of the plantations that cloak the hinterland of Rivock Edge, which only shows its true face to the Keighley side. Beyond the trees the Aire Valley leads the eye to the South Pennine landmarks of Earl Crag and Pinhaw Beacon, with the great whaleback of Pendle Hill, in Lancashire, beyond. Northwards are many peaks of the southern Dales, with Buckden Pike and Great Whernside prominent.* On leaving, note the broader path just below you, doubling back right to drop ever slightly along the moor, its intermittent moist moments largely much better than the outward path. This runs on to reach Cowper's Cross. *A cowper was a dealer, and it seems this was a market cross brought from elsewhere, later converted to a true cross.* Fifty yards further is Keighley Road again.

Turn left down here to reach a green knoll above the amphitheatre of Grainings Head, revealing Ilkley again. Just yards further as it swings left, take a path straight ahead, dropping through bracken close by Spicey Gill on the right. Passing above an old grassed-over quarry rim on your right, then over a contouring cross-path, it drops quite steeply to rejoin the road which by now is surfaced. Continue down to a parking area at the base of the moor alongside Spicey Gill. *Just before it on your left is an old guidepost inscribed to Keighley and Ilkley, complete with carved hands.* Cross the bridge, then at once leave by a path contouring right through the bracken from a small parking area. This runs a splendid course across the moor, losing a little height and also absorbing a path from the left, but foolproof as White Wells is seen ahead. Further on you join the stony service road rising to White Wells. Turn left down this back to the road, and right to finish. *Immediately on your left is Wells House, built in 1856 as one of a number of hydropathic establishments catering for the demand for curing ailments by means of liberal contact with the cold waters that sprang from the moor.*

COW & CALF ROCKS

A rich tapestry of fascinating landmarks, both natural and man-made, are scattered on and about Burley Moor

START *Ilkley (SE 117471; LS29 9JN)*

DISTANCE *6$\frac{1}{2}$ miles (10$\frac{1}{2}$km)*

ORDNANCE SURVEY 1:25,000 MAP
Explorer 297 - Lower Wharfedale & Washburn Valley

ACCESS *Start from Darwin Gardens car park immediately above moor-foot cattle-grid at top of Wells Road, which climbs steeply from The Grove. Buses and rail station in town centre.*
•OPEN ACCESS - dogs on leads on Burley Moor, March to July.

Rejoin the road and cross the cattle-grid on your left, then immediately double back right to rise to a gate set back from a small parking area. Bear left on the surfaced driveway rising away. It quickly veers away from the wall and rises to shortly arrive at The Tarn. A surfaced path runs around both sides, and at the far end a few steps send a path away across the moor. This rapidly merges into a broader one coming up from the left, and now runs on and rises to drop to a footbridge on lively Backstone Beck.

Across the stream take the gentler graded left fork rising away. At quite an early fork keep right, aiming for the right side of the trees above. Rising more steeply past an inscribed pointed boulder you reach a cross-paths at the edge of the trees. Remain on the main path into the scattered plantation. This slants up and out of the edge of the trees to a fork at the start of the massive former Hangingstone Quarries on your right. Keep left below a bouldery knoll through the last few trees, and at a major fork ignore that dropping left as your path rises to emerge behind the Cow & Calf Rocks. Advance straight on to the crest, being aware of the drop!

The Cow & Calf Rocks constitute one of Yorkshire's premier landmarks: until modern day romanticism they were the Hanging Stones. This is a hugely popular climbing area, with substantial rock-faces easy of access. The main buttress of the Cow, however, is so bold and uncompromising that most climbers will be found in the great bowl of the quarry round the back, with the added advantage of a south-facing outlook to put the sun on their backs. Below the Cow is its off-spring the Calf, whose scooped steps offer an easy angled scramble for the casual visitor.

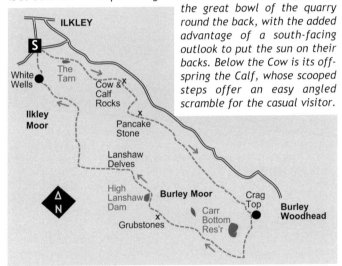

Bear right along the top, past the gaping climbers' quarry to a firmer path, quickly reaching a broad cross-paths at the end of the rocks. The left branch drops to a popular car park, café and the Cow & Calf Hotel. Cross straight over along a firm, level path. After 150 yards keep on over a cross-path, and after a further 100 yards, with the shapely Pancake Stone on the skyline ahead, another path junction is reached just before a fork. Turn right here for a short, grassy ascent towards a skyline nick, then take the path left to begin a splendid march along this modest edge. *Wharfedale views look across to Middleton and Denton Moors, and down-dale to Otley, Almscliff Crag and Otley Chevin.* Shortly you arrive just above the Pancake Stone, to which a branch drops left. *Its flat top is awash with cup marks, Bronze Age in origin but exact purpose unknown.*

The onward path passes yellow-topped posts indicating arrival on Burley Moor. The path drops a little to merge with a broader, grassy one from below. Small quarries sit to your left, and the path drops gently to a streamlet crossing and up again to a wall corner. Forge on with the wall, dropping gently again, and just after the wall turns off, you arrive above the steeper drop to Coldstone Beck. The path descends to cross the stony stream.

Doubling back left to a fork, take the rougher upper one a few feet to emerge onto the level. Head directly away, ignoring a very early left branch, then straight on over a cross-path to rise very slightly, aiming for a solitary dwelling at Crag Top. Pass right of an old quarry to join a moor-edge access track in front of the house. Turn right, rising past York View Farm and ignoring a flagged track right to Carr Bottom Reservoir, remain on this. It rises past one further house (Carr Bottom) to bend sharp left at a wall corner. Here rise straight up the moor in front, rapidly joining a shooters' track rising from the left. Turn right on its fenceside course, rising past a boundary stone. Carr Bottom Reservoir sits just down to the right. *Now on the broad watershed, views over Airedale to the left feature Emley Moor and Holme Moss masts and Ovenden Moor windfarm. To your right over Wharfedale are the Menwith Hill radomes and Knabs Ridge windfarm, with Lower Lanshaw Dam below. Man's hand is so clumsy on the landscape!*

The track is a delight as it continually rises, leaving the fence to run by a line of grouse butts before reaching a wooden shooters' cabin at the Grubstones. *Easily missed yet simply located is Grubstones stone circle, lurking in the heather just 60 yards along a thin trod behind the cabin. Some 10 major stones of this burial cairn survive within a 10 yards diameter.* On a knoll just beyond the hut are the Grubstones. *This cluster of boulders makes a fine viewpoint and a great spot to linger.* Back on the track, advance just a short way further down to a dip, where a grassy path bears off right to drop to High Lanshaw Dam. Across the old outflow the path runs along the embankment. At the path junction at the end, drop immediately left on a path to stepping-stones over a marsh, then rising gently away to a post on a knoll at the start of Lanshaw Delves. Here the path forks, your way being the more inviting left branch. *The delves are a distinctive line of small-scale quarries, identified by a long line of shallow hollows. The second contains the recumbent Lanshaw Lass boundary stone, inscribed 'ILB'.*

A super path runs a dead-level course the length of the delves, and at the end reverts to a moister moorland path for the short continuation to meet the flagged Dick Hudson's path. Turn right for a splendid descent across Ilkley Moor. Crossing bouldery Backstone Beck the flags end and the path forks. Keep to the left one rising briefly before continuing a steady descent. Soon reaching a major cross-paths, go straight over. With Ilkley re-appearing the path drops left to the western rim of Ilkley Crags. The path then drops steeply and roughly left before resuming in broad, easy mode to wind down to the rear of White Wells. *For a note on White Wells see page 21.* From the front a partly stepped path drops down through colourful terrain to return to the moor-gate where you began.

Sheep gathering at Grubstones, Burley Moor

AROUND MIDDLETON

Rich rural delights just across the Wharfe from Ilkley

START *Ilkley (SE 112480; LS29 9EU)*

DISTANCE *7^{1}4 miles (11^{1}2km)*

ORDNANCE SURVEY 1:25,000 MAP
Explorer 297 - Lower Wharfedale & Washburn Valley

ACCESS *Start from the Old Bridge at upstream end of riverside park. Car parks, buses and rail station in town centre.*

For a note on Ilkley, see page 20. The Old Bridge was rebuilt after a great flood of 1673 that swept away many of the Wharfe's bridges. Happily it has long been left for pedestrian use, and the walk concludes by crossing it. Follow the Wharfe downstream past the Riverside Hotel, rowing boats and playground. *These green spaces are the townsfolk's memorial to their fallen in World War Two.* An underpass takes you beneath the modern road bridge. *Opened in 1904, it replaced a ferry that supported the Old Bridge.* Continue downstream on this urban path nudged by suburbia onto a quieter section to a suspension footbridge on the Wharfe.

Cross to the Denton road under Stubham Wood and resume downstream, using some verges parallel with the Wharfe passing a drive to the Nell Bank Centre. Just beyond, at a stile on the left, cross to the far corner of a field, then along a fieldside below trees to a kissing-gate onto Carters Lane. Take the drive to Beckfoot

Farm opposite, and crossing a bridge into the yard, go straight ahead past the garden. *A relocated Middleton/Denton boundary stone stands by the garden wall.* Turn left outside the wall along a path on a grassy brow to a small gate in the boundary wall. At this original site of the stone, escape into a sylvan paradise. Cross and bear right outside West Park Wood. Beyond two stiles/gates a track out of the wood runs on through two further fields to a gate/stile onto a road. Turn up its leafy course into the tiny village of Denton.

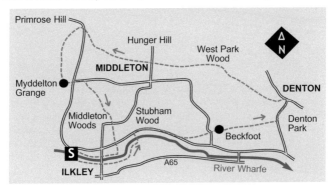

For a note on Denton, see page 31. Turn left at the tiny green to quickly find a stile/gate onto a short enclosed track on the left. From a stile/gate at the end advance with a fence to the top of West Park Wood. A stile/gate keep you out of the trees, running along the top to one giving access into the far end, as the wood starts to curve right. Path and bridge combine to see you out via a stile. Cross a large, sloping field enveloped by woodland to a stile into trees, and a path descends to a footbridge on Bow Beck and steeply up the bank. Bearing right at a kink at the top the path runs through the wood-edge. On leaving the trees at a stile the way traces a fence rising gently away. Interrupted by a farm track and another stile, the next stile sends steps down to a tiny footbridge, then cross to a stile onto Hunger Hill Lane. From a stile opposite head past a house: stiles either end of an unkempt enclosure send you away with a wall. From a stile at the end forge on with a winding wall, and towards the end of this large field slant up to a gate opposite. *During this spell the widest views yet feature the spread of Rombalds Moor.*

Continue slanting up and across to a fence-stile, and rise again to the opposite corner to emerge via a stile onto a bend of Hardings Lane at Primrose Hill. *This ascending road on the walk's summit is on the line of the Roman road from Ilkley to Boroughbridge.* Cross to a gate opposite and head down the fieldside. Past the top of a plantation pass through a gate onto a cart track, then turn left on it through a gate in a wall. It descends pleasantly to a wood edge and joins a drive. *Immersed in woodland 200 yards to the right is Calvary, within the grounds of Myddelton Lodge (now Myddelton Grange). Created around 1850, carved stones representing the Stations of the Cross line a path to a grotto.*

The drive descends past cottages to swing left back onto Hardings Lane. *Myddelton Grange is a Roman Catholic pastoral centre. It was rebuilt around 1600 by William Middleton, whose family resided here as influential Catholics until the estate was passed to the church. The chapel was built in 1854, and for 50 years Ilkley folk climbed the hill to worship until a church was built in the town. The imposing gritstone house sports mullioned and transomed windows, while modern buildings alongside help fulfil its modern-day role.*

On Hardings Lane, turn left to a junction. *On the left stands a very old guidepost whose destinations include Rip(p)on.* Here branch right along the Middleton lane. Past a solitary house take a stile on the right, and slant left down the field to a stile into Middleton Woods. *In spring a carpet of bluebells decorate the wood.* An immediate fork is the first of many twists and turns: go right, then immediately left at another fork to descend a little before running left to a junction. Keep right on the main path, descending a steep flight of stone steps, then continuing down more gently. Towards the bottom it runs left over a tiny footbridge just beyond a crossroads with a thinner path. At the next fork keep right, dropping down a finger of woodland between houses to emerge via a kissing-gate onto a suburban avenue.

Go briefly left to descend a few steps to playing fields at the open-air pool. Suddenly you're back in the thick of things, and on a nice day there'll be people slurping ice cream and picnicking amongst numerous sporting attractions. Pass the pool on your left to cross a road, on past the rugby ground to the riverbank. Go right to cross the new bridge to return by the Wharfe to the Old Bridge.

DENTON MOOR

A lengthy climb through fields to spacious moorland heights

START *Denton (SE 143489; LS29 0HG)*

DISTANCE *6$\frac{1}{2}$ miles (10$\frac{1}{2}$km)*

ORDNANCE SURVEY 1:25,000 MAP
Explorer 297 - Lower Wharfedale & Washburn Valley

ACCESS *Start from the village centre, small roadside parking area by phonebox. Rail station a long mile distant at Ben Rhydding.*
•OPEN ACCESS - short section on track preferable to invisible path.

Denton is a tiny village backwater far removed from Ilkley across the valley. The old school stands back from a tiny triangular green. Along to the right past Home Farm is Denton Hall. In 1515 the old hall became, for around 200 years, home to one of Yorkshire's famous families, when Sir William Fairfax married a daughter of the Thwaites family. Sir - later Lord - Thomas Fairfax was a major figure in the Civil War, a soldier who led Parliamentarian forces in numerous clashes, greatest being the Battle of Marston Moor in 1644. The present hall dates from around 1770: designed by John Carr of York, it is currently an events venue. Before the hall is St Helen's church. By the same architect and entirely unspoilt, it dates from 1776 and was a private chapel until becoming the parish church in 1867. It enjoys a sequestered rural setting, and possesses a rare stained glass window removed from the old hall.

31

Facing the tiny green, go right then immediately left at the fork on Smithy Lane heading past cottages. Just after a modern barn complex, as the road steepens, take a stile on the left and head directly up the field centre. Levelling out at the top, advance to a stile just ahead. Resume rising more gently with a wall, and through a gate at the top rise alongside a streamlet to absorb a grass track to reach Willow Hill Farm. Continue straight up outside its confines and along to a gate just across the streamlet. Keep on towards the big modern barn complex at Yarnett House Farm, then go left with a fence. Part way along pass through a gate in it, and another in the fence behind. Bear right up the field centre to find a stile in the sturdy wall at the top. *This is a good place to look back at the expanding views over the valley to the full girth of Rombalds Moor.*

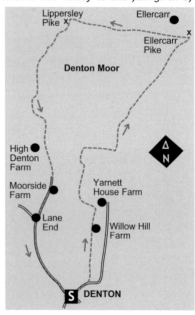

Bear left away from it, dropping slightly to two corner gates just left of a small wood. From the left one advance the short way with the wall to join a firm cart track. Turn right up this, and over a cattle-grid at the top, leave by a gate on the right. Cross a field bottom to a gate at the foot of a strip plantation, and resume across a larger field bottom, rising to a gate in the wall ahead. Joining an invisible old way turn left past a dewpond to a corner gate just ahead. *Your path is an old trading route known as Low Badger Gate, 'badger' being an old term for a corn dealer.*

Through this take the gate on your left and resume with the wall on your right. Through a gate in a fence, advance to a gap in the trees ahead. The gate here puts you onto a corner of Denton Moor.

A grassy path bears right to a fence beneath a strip plantation edge, then follows the gently rising fence across the moor. *Wooded Norwood Edge and its mast are seen over to the right as more of the Washburn Valley appears.* This largely super path through the heather ultimately arrives - just after the fence turns off - at a gate at another moorland corner on Ellercarr Pike. *Menwith Hill radomes appear as you gain it. An access road to the isolated house of Eller Carr is through the gate, though you need only use it to inspect a pair of boundary stones on this grassy knoll. The taller one inscribed 'D' and 'A' refers to the parishes of Denton and Askwith, while the shorter one is inscribed '9 KF 1825': this refers to its position on the boundary of the historic Forest of Knaresborough.*

Remaining on the moor, turn left on the wallside path (High Badger Gate) aiming for the dome of Lippersley Pike. The path heads across the heathery upper reaches of Denton Moor, with several moist sections to circumvent. With Timble Ings plantation over the wall on the right, the path rises gently towards the heathery spur of Lippersley Ridge. Just past a Denton boundary stone, ignore a branch right to the plantation corner. Your way mounts the ridge to another boundary stone where a path crosses yours at an angle. Remain on the main path rising to yet another boundary stone, with the big cairn at 1082ft/330m on Lippersley Pike appearing just two minutes further. *This proves to be hollow, and the OS map denotes it as a cairn of antiquity. Alongside is another Forest boundary stone inscribed '11 KF 1767': this is one of 49 numbered stones erected at the time of the Enclosures, marking the limits of a hunting forest dating back to at least Norman times.*

Leave by a path on the left some 20 paces before the cairn - not the path between cairn and boundary stone. This drops briefly steeply to bear left to the start of a line of grouse butts. Running alongside these it broadens before meeting a shooters' track to drop down to a stone shooting cabin just ahead. Simply continue down this superb grassy track, dropping left at the bottom to a corner stile by a gate off the moor. The track continues grandly down a wallside by colourful gorse to a gate at the bottom, joining an access road from High Denton Farm. Simply remain on its pleasant, traffic-free course as it becomes a public road, passing Moorside Farm and down to a junction at the former Lane End Farm. Continue down Bore Hill to descend back into Denton.

WALK 8 OTLEY CHEVIN

A thorough exploration of an iconic Wharfedale landmark featuring woodland, moorland, outcrops and massive views

START *Otley (SE 201455; LS21 3AQ)*

DISTANCE *6^{1}2 miles (10^{1}2km)*

ORDNANCE SURVEY 1:25,000 MAP
Explorer 297 - Lower Wharfedale & Washburn Valley

ACCESS *Start from the town centre. Car parks.
Bus from Leeds, Ilkley, Keighley, Harrogate*

The buzzing little market town of Otley sits on the south bank of the Wharfe, and throws a long, sturdy bridge across the wide flowing river. In this birthplace of celebrated cabinet-maker Thomas Chippendale, mid-May sees the colourful Otley Show herald the start of the county's 'show' season. A summer evening in early July sees the streets closed for a prestigious series of cycle races, and they're closed again in December for a very popular Victorian market. At All Saints church a memorial based on the portal of the nearby Bramhope rail tunnel honours lives lost in its construction. The Jacobean former grammar school is centrally placed, while Otley remains proud of its wealth of public houses. A livestock auction mart serves the district's farmers, while the small square still hosts weekly markets beneath a clock tower of 1887 built to commemorate Queen Victoria's Golden Jubilee.

From the clock tower head left along Kirkgate. At the junction outside the parish church go right on Burras Lane, and follow this suburban road all the way to a T-junction with West Chevin Road. Go left over the by-pass (cynically built on the course of the old railway) and bear right on its footway as it rises out of town. After a short while, with open fields on the right, leave by a path signed through steps on the left. This rises into open country, between a fence and a small wooded streamlet. This sustained climb moves between trees and clearings before swinging right to slant up into more trees. This culminates in wooden steps between boulders near the top edge of the wood. At this path junction take that slanting steadily uphill to the left, up the right side of a beech 'clearing' then left along what is almost the wood top.

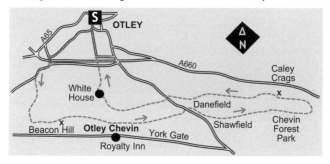

Three massive boulders mark the start of a gentle rise inside the wood beneath a line of crags. At the end a wall replaces the fence and you arrive at a wood edge corner. *Big views look south-wards to distant Emley Moor and Holme Moss.* At the path junction here advance straight on with an attractive pond down to your right. At the end of this ignore a left branch and keep on to leave the trees for a grand open course along the moor top. *Massive views look back up-dale to Rombalds Moor, Barden Moor and Simon's Seat.* Another junction is quickly reached. *Unseen just to your right is Yorkgate Quarry, while a right branch passes above it to a heathery knoll that forms the Chevin's anonymous high point.* Your onward path drops marginally to merge with a path coming in from the left. Running on, remain beneath a wall to quickly gain the crest of the rocks along the top of Beacon Hill Moor.

This eminent vantage point boasts a fine panorama, with identification of features aided by the presence of a rangefinder on the Beacon House site. With distances in miles, it picks out man-made creations such as the masts on Emley Moor 20 and Holme Moss 26, York Minster 26, Arthington Viaduct 4, Kilburn White Horse 30, and Ferrybridge Power Station 21. Distant natural features include Great Whernside high in the Yorkshire Dales and Boulsworth Hill on the Lancashire border. Nearer to hand across the Wharfe are more regular contributions from the local area, including Farnley Hall, Denton and Middleton Moors, and Beamsley Beacon – not to mention the bird's-eye view of Otley itself.

The Beacon House, known as Jenny's Cottage after one of its former occupants, was finally fully demolished in 1976. This has been the setting for many a bonfire, either to warn of historic approaching danger or more usually to celebrate happy, invariably royal, events. It is also the location of a great wooden cross, around 30ft in height, erected annually to mark the start of Holy Week leading up to Easter. Its siting is clearly visible to townsfolk in the streets below.

The path resumes to pass the ever busy Surprise View car park just below. *The Royalty pub is just two minutes away at this point, while the car park often has an ice cream van.* When the broad wallside path becomes flagged, ignore the left branch slanting away and keep on past gorse and heather. The wall soon ends and the path crosses a small patch of open ground before firming up again to arrive at Miller Lane Gate. Here you leave the moor and follow Miller Lane, a stony, gently descending track to reach East Chevin Road. Cross to a gap opposite into the woods of Danefield: a splendid path rises to the right, parallel with the road to reach Shawfield car park. *This last section is awash with spring-time bluebells.*

Turn left into Chevin Forest Park and head directly away on the main, broad track into the trees. Dropping gently away it then rises to a big junction beyond a streamlet, where advance straight on. *A broad grassy break part way on offers an optional short-cut down onto the lower path on the crest of Caley Crags.* Eventually you arrive at a major junction with an open area ahead. From a kissing-gate on your left, a broad path curves left down through open country to the crest of the lower grouping of Caley Crags. *This is a fine place to linger, looking over the boulders. Down below is Pool's busy bridge over the Wharfe, with Almscliff Crag across the valley.*

Resume left on the crest, and deeper in trees a kissing-gate puts you onto a broader path. Keep straight on, passing the scant ruins of Keeper's Cottage. At a major fork take the upper path, climbing briefly to gain the dramatic crest of the main grouping of Caley Crags. *These walls of rock plunge dramatically from close to the path, and are often festooned with climbers.* Resuming, the path drops a little to a junction just before a footbridge. Don't cross it but turn steeply down a narrow path on the right thirty yards earlier to join the lower track at a crossroads. Go left to bridge the gill. *A little further along, a bracken clearing below is the site of an Iron Age settlement.* The splendid way runs through the glorious bluebell surrounds of Danefield nature reserve. Ignore both a permissive bridleway climbing left, and also a branch right just before a short rise to emerge back onto East Chevin Road at Danefield Gate. *All the land on this side of the road was the Danefield estate and Caley Deer Park of Farnley Hall, presented to the town in 1946 by Major Horton-Fawkes as a memorial to Otley's war dead.*

Turn up the footway for 100 yards and cross to East Chevin Quarry car park. Part way along, a broad path climbs away to run beneath quarried cliffs, easing out before moorland slopes are revealed below. *These form a colourful foreground to Otley on the valley floor.* Further, woodland is re-entered and the path meets a broad track descending from the foot of Beacon Hill Moor. Bear right down this, deeper into woodland to shortly arrive at the White House. *This former farmhouse is now a visitor centre, with refreshments and WCs (when open). It has long been a haunt of visitors and picnickers, though one must go round the front to appreciate its name. It is normally open weekend afternoons April-October, Sundays in November, December, and possibly March.* Take the broad path on its far side, winding down through trees to a gate onto an access road. Crossing straight over, an enclosed, surfaced path descends between trees and fields to emerge onto a road, Birdcage Walk. Cross straight over to a footbridge over the by-pass, putting you onto the end of Station Road which heads away to emerge back in the centre.

NETHERBY DEEP

A splendid, sustained length of riverbank, with history too

START *Weeton (SE 286468; LS17 0AY)*

DISTANCE *7³⁄4 miles (12¹⁄2km)*

ORDNANCE SURVEY 1:25,000 MAP
Explorer 289 - Leeds **or**
Explorer 297 - Lower Wharfedale & Washburn Valley

ACCESS *Start from the village centre. Roadside parking on Main Street (or Brook Lane). Weeton station is almost a mile distant at Huby, on Leeds-Harrogate line.*

Weeton is an attractive, sleepy village tucked away near the Wharfe, between the busy Harrogate-Bradford and Harrogate-Leeds roads. At the central junction is a spacious green, with the Old Hall set back behind an old Methodist chapel. Just back along the street is the old schoolhouse. Further still is the church of St Barnabus, whose spire dominates the local landscape, the work of renowned architect Giles Gilbert Scott. A churchyard memorial recalls the victims of a plane crash at nearby Dunkeswick in 1995.

Facing the old chapel, turn right along the street until you reach Brook Lane on the left. Follow this suburban cul-de-sac almost to its demise, where an enclosed path on the right runs to a bridle-gate onto a drive at a cluster of buildings. Turn left through a gate between buildings then sharp right between stables, and straight on to a tall wooden gate. This accesses a footbridge on tiny Weeton Beck to escape into a large field, then rise to the top left corner. *Wide views look back over the village to Bramhope, also to Almscliff Crag.* From a stile continue up the steep little fieldside outside a wood and along to a stile onto a narrow lane. *By now you have extensive views eastwards over the Wharfe Valley.*

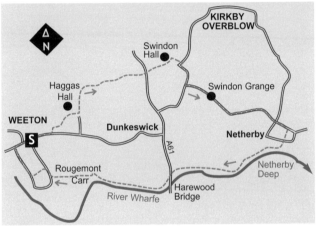

Go left along the lane, at once losing its surface as a branch goes left to Haggas Hall. Ignore this and keep straight on the grassy track of Green Lane, running a splendid course through lush foliage onto Healthwaite Hill. Remain on the track as it turns sharp right beneath a mast, enjoying another dead straight march as it drops gently to the A61 road. From a bridle-gate opposite, bear gently right across the field to a bridle-gate at the bottom, accessing a grassy, stone-arched bridge on Keswick Beck. Across, rise away along a hedgeside to a corner gate, from where a grassy track runs to the farm at Swindon Hall. Bear right to pass outside the tall garden wall of the house, through a gate and past fine gateposts. *These are all that remain of a Jacobean hall that replaced the original medieval house, destroyed by Royalists during the Civil War: the present hall dates from the 1830s.* Advance to join the access road just ahead. *On the left here are the banks of an old moat that surrounded the original hall.* The drive leads down onto a road, Swindon Lane.

Here begins around a mile and a half of road walking. *Largely traffic-free, it gives wide views with Kirkby Overblow on its ridge to the left, the Wharfe Valley outspread right, and the likelihood of a display of red kites soaring overhead. On my visit one poor bird was being continually mobbed by an irksome crow.* Turn right past Swindon Lodge to a junction, and go left on unsigned Spring Lane. *Autumn sees the adjacent hedges ablaze with the colours of seasonal fruit, including elderberry, sloe, blackberry and hawthorn.* The road leads on past two farms to a crossroads watched over by an old West Riding roadsign. Go straight across, but immediately after Springmoor Lodge on the right, take a path down the side of a chalet site. Squeezing (sometimes tightly) by the rear of a string of chalets, it emerges into an open area, deflected right of wooden huts and then down again to a small gate at the bottom onto narrow Wharfe Lane through Netherby.

Go left a few paces then turn right through a gate at Wharfe Hill Farm, and along a grassy track that bears right behind the buildings. This runs briefly upstream to the bank of the Wharfe at Netherby Deep. *At this sandy beach is the site of an old ford, and a notice of a past tragedy is a reminder of the dangers of the river hereabouts.* A good path takes over, crossing a footbridge on a sidestream and then running along the field edge, with good breaks in the trees to enjoy the river. At the end the path is deflected from the river to find a footbridge on a tiny sidestream. Across, bear left to rejoin the riverbank path and resume upstream, at the end meeting a green track coming in from the right. This runs on into a few trees, but as it turns away, keep straight on the broad riverbank continuation. This is a splendid section of path, neatly enclosed between river and hedgerow. Ultimately this broadens and rises as a track to run on past the housing development of Bridge Court to meet the A61 again, at Harewood Bridge.

Cross the road and go left, briefly, but immediately before the bridge take a gate into the yard of a house. A corner kissing-gate puts you back onto the riverbank, with the sturdy bridge to your left. The next stage is again a grand one, as lush pasture leads on past a wide, breached weir. *This served a mill on the opposite bank, while over to the right rises Almscliff Crag.* On your right are rusting remain of a sluice. Reaching a stile the path delves into a little undergrowth with a pond, and continues on the bank before entering trees. A plank bridge crosses a streamlet to a few wooden steps, and on through trees the path soon ascends wooden steps to a field edge. This is farewell to the Wharfe, so resume along the fieldside to the edge of the woodland at Rougemont Carr. Turning right outside the wood, the path quickly turns through an ancient bank into the trees. *Springtime sees a spectacular bluebell display throughout these woods.* Remain on this main path as it bears right and winds on to a junction in the trees. Close by on your left is the very distinct Rougemont embankment. *Perhaps dating back to Anglo-Saxon times, this was also the site of a castle of the Lords de L'Isle some 700 years ago.* Keep straight on (left) to forge on through the wood, initially with the old embankment parallel to your left.

A bridle-gate at the end of the wood (with bank and ditch again evident) puts you into a lush field, with Weeton's church spire ahead. Bear left to a bridle-gate in the facing hedge, just short of the corner: this accesses a packhorse bridge on Weeton Beck. Across, advance to join a track and follow this right past sewage works. Faced with two gates, take the left one from where a track runs out onto narrow Gallogate Lane. Turn right on this to return to the village centre. If visiting the church, advance only as far as the end of the first field, and take a stile in the hedge on the left. Cross two fieldsides to a stile onto the western loop of Gallogate Lane. Again turn right, and this leads by the church and then on to a T-junction, where turn right to finish back in the village.

Harewood Bridge

HAREWOOD PARK

Undemanding walking through a famous parkland landscape

START *Harewood (SE 320452; LS17 9LJ)*

DISTANCE *5³4 miles (9¹4km)*

ORDNANCE SURVEY 1:25,000 MAP
Explorer 289 - Leeds **or**
Explorer 297 - Lower Wharfedale & Washburn Valley

ACCESS *Start from the village centre. Village hall car park on Church Lane (donation box). Leeds-Harrogate bus.*

Harewood is a model estate village outside the entrance to Harewood House, one of Yorkshire's premier stately homes. Other features include the Harewood Arms, a Post office/shop, and the remains of what began as a 12th century Norman castle. Harewood House is the seat of the Earl of Harewood, a title first bestowed in 1812 on Edwin Lascelles whose family came over with William the Conqueror. Dating from 1759, Harewood House was built on profits of the Lascelles' West Indian sugar plantations. It boasts an unrivalled pedigree, being designed by John Carr, with interiors by Robert Adam, furniture by Chippendale, and grounds courtesy of Capability Brown. Victorian architect Charles Barry was responsible for the third storey, and created an Italianate terrace along the south facade. The resplendent rooms are notable for housing an extensive fine art collection alongside outstanding furnishings.

Within the grounds is a bird garden and woodland and lakeside walks, while special interest events take place throughout the year. Herds of deer are likely to be encountered roaming the grounds, while the successful release of red kites has resulted in these magnificent birds of prey being a permanent sight soaring above the grounds. From the village hall (with café) keep straight on Church Lane, becoming a private road passing right of a lodge. This runs on between woods to emerge into the open. *The Wharfe Valley prospect features the landmarks of Norwood Edge and Almscliff Crag.* A short detour goes left on a walled track to enter All Saints churchyard. *Set amid a rolling sea of springtime bluebells, the now redundant church dates from the 15th century. Within are six magnificent 15th century alabaster tombs, all in pairs and featuring either the Gascoigne family or the Lords of Harewood.*

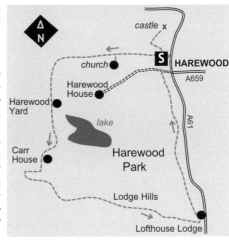

Back on the access road, resume along the brow. The road drops to a bridleway crossroads, where the main one runs left along an open pasture to Harewood Yard. *The site of Home Farm is now a tasteful conversion to offices.* Advance straight on, through a gate and down another access road to bridge Stank Beck by a pond. Keep straight on up a rough road, joining another from the left and rising briefly steeply past a house. A little further, bear right at a fork to descend past a tall red-brick wall. Through a cattle-grid at the bottom, keep right at another fork through a belt of trees. This rises outside Carr Wood to Carr House. Past the house a continuing track rises into trees and swings right. During this steady rise, look out for a sunken track doubling back left up to a track crossroads.

Turn left along the level track through fine woodland. *A cluster of stone buildings just visible over the wall is the purpose-built set of TV soap 'Emmerdale'.* The track runs grandly on for some time before dropping to bridge a streamlet, then it swings left to a major junction. Go left to the graceful, stone-arched New Bridge, just ahead. Turn right over this and the track leaves the trees to rise in grand style through open parkland. *This delectable rolling landscape soon offers a view back to the house.* A sustained rise precedes a high, level course over Lodge Hills to pass through a gate to approach large entrance gates at Lofthouse Lodge, now replaced by a large house. *These last few minutes offer a better proportioned view of the majestic frontage of Harewood House.*

Beyond the gates is the busy A61 Leeds-Harrogate road, but this is neatly avoided by the permissive Wallside Path which remains within the grounds: dogs must be on leads here. *The path can occasionally be closed for short periods, in this unlikely event the alternative would be to tramp the last mile along the road.* Turn left in front of the house and drop to a gate into Wall Side Plantation. The broad path runs a splendid course, never far from the high wall that keeps you from the invisible though audible traffic. Ultimately the broadening track emerges alongside estate sheds on your right. Bear left on the track a short way as it curves around to join the main driveway to the house. Turn right on this to emerge back onto the road in style through the main gateway arch. *With lodges at either side this grandiose gateway dates from 1804.* Go left on the footway the short way back to Church Lane.

A detour to see the castle is quickly accomplished. A path leaves the far corner of the car park to run past garages and emerge on the end of suburban Bondgate. Go right as far as a bend right for the main road, then take a short driveway on the left to find a tall-walled path descending beneath a 15 yards-long tunnel into trees. Turning right you arrive at an information panel alongside a ha-ha. From here a permissive path runs to the castle. Simply follow the good path alongside the ditch for a few minutes to arrive beneath the ruin: steps and stepping-stones give access. Ascend the path on its left side, and passing along the top side a good path heads back through the trees. At a fork take the right branch to slant down the short way back to the information panel, where cross the ditch in similar style to earlier, and retrace steps.

Delectable fieldpaths seek out a lovely old church

START *Leathley (SE 232470; LS21 2JU)*

DISTANCE *6³⁄4 miles (10³⁄4km)*

ORDNANCE SURVEY 1:25,000 MAP
Explorer 297 - Lower Wharfedale & Washburn Valley

ACCESS *Start from the roadside brow opposite church on B6161. Small parking area with donation box.*

Scattered Leathley is centred on St Oswald's church, with its magnificent Norman tower and nave. A Norman door is decorated with ironwork, while the mouse symbol of the Kilburn workshops is found on items of furniture. Also on this brow are the picturesque almshouses and old school, founded in 1769. Turn north on the B6161 footway, passing a turnpike milestone amid exclusive properties. On reaching Mill House (former Leathley Mill) at the foot of the hill, turn left on an enclosed path outside the grounds to emerge at the goit that supplied it. A path heads away with the River Washburn to your left: a potentially moist section soon reaches a stile. Just fifty yards further at the river bend, bear right to rise back to the dry goit. Bear left on its tree-lined course, through a field then via a gate and a stile as it takes on a wet course outside a fish farm which it has been restored to supply. Cross the drive and resume along to stone steps up onto a road at Lindley Bridge.

Turn right, and just past a lodge on the bend, a path is signed left on a very short driveway. At the gate a briefly enclosed path turns up to a stile into a field. A sustained climb up Lindley Warren bears away from the fieldside to an outer wall corner. *Colourful slopes offer good views back over to Otley Chevin.* This nice ascent continues to a gate at the top by houses at Lindley Green. Don't pass through but follow the wallside path left, through a hand-gate to a stile onto an access road. *This stage affords a good view over Lindley Wood Reservoir backed by Rombalds Moor.* Turn right up this the short way to a road at Lindley Green.

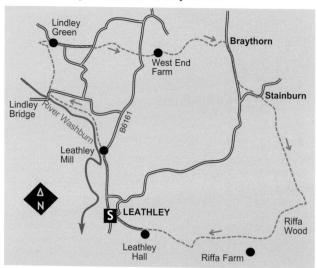

Bear right along the road, noting an old kiln in the field above. Keep left at a fork, rising a little to the high point of the walk with far-reaching Wharfe Valley views. At a T-junction cross straight over to follow the top side of a sloping field opposite. *Though the map suggests the other side of the fence, there's no way through it further on.* In the second field bear right to contour across to a tall wall-stile. Contour across the next large, sloping field to locate a stile at the right end of the section of wall ahead. Again cross straight over the B6161 and along the drive to West End Farm.

Without entering the yard take a stile on the left to begin a circuit of the farm's perimeter. From a corner stile go right to a gate just outside the yard. An enclosed track heads away to a gate into a field: don't pass through, but from a stile on its left follow a short, L-shaped wooded path around to a bridle-gate into the field. From a wall-stile on the left head away with a fence on your left, dropping gently to a corner stile. Now drop left down the field to a stile onto the enclosed old pathway of Gale Lane. Turn right on its slender course, dropping to bridge West Beck. Rising away more spaciously, a lovely stroll swings left to rise onto Church Lane in Braythorn, emerging alongside a former Methodist Chapel of 1836.

Turn right through the hamlet, and within a few minutes you arrive at a gate into Stainburn church. *In the care of the Churches Conservation Trust, St Mary's is a lovely church dating from Norman times.* The surfaced path continues to a corner kissing-gate, from where slant down a wallside to another onto a road in the hamlet of Stainburn. Turn left the short way down to the lowest point.

In the dip take a gate on the right and a good track heads away. Underfoot for some time, this splendid route bridges then follows tiny East Beck. After a brief walled section it emerges to bridge the stream, then runs on the field boundary side to re-cross it a little further on. This time the track leaves it on a green course slanting left up to a gate in a fence. As a less defined green way it runs along field tops beneath a hedge, continuing more faintly to a stile/gate at the end. Now contour across a field to a gate at the corner of Riffa Wood. Advance on outside the trees, quickly taking a hand-gate on the right to follow a stone causey down through the wood. *Copious bluebells decorate this attractive woodland.*

At the bottom leave by another hand-gate and advance to stepping-stones on West Beck. Up the bank behind, bear left across the field centre to a gate at the start of an enclosed track, Hall Lane. Now simply follow this same, largely enclosed way all the way back. After an early branch drops left to Riffa Farm a superb grassy way takes over, reaching a gentle brow on Leafield Bank. Dropping to a gate, a part moist, sunken section leads down to a corner stile. Swinging right it now runs enclosed all the way, a super path that becomes a cart track running on to Leathley Hall. *Dating from the early 18th century, its attractive frontage is well seen as you pass.* The access road is absorbed to run out the short way to the start.

LINDLEY WOOD

Riverbank, reservoir, wood, pasture - and a famous bridge

START *Farnley (SE 224483; LS21 2QN)*

DISTANCE *6³⁄4 miles (10³⁄4km)*

ORDNANCE SURVEY 1:25,000 MAP
Explorer 297 - Lower Wharfedale & Washburn Valley

ACCESS *Start from Lindley Bridge, on Cinder Lane a half-mile off B6451 east of Farnley. Parking area on west side of bridge.*

Lindley is a scattered farming community, with Lindley Farm on the road from the B6161 serving as 'Emmerdale Farm' in the TV soap's earlier years. Looking upstream from the bridge is a mill goit, restored to serve a fishery immediately downstream. From the bridge head west up the road, rising gently before swinging steeply uphill to ease out before meeting the B6451 at Farnley. *On your right is the old school, closed in 2013.* Cross to the footway and turn right a short way to the church. *Modest All Saints church was rebuilt in 1851.* Just a few strides further along the road, pass a cottage and go left on Haddockstones farm drive. *This offers views over to Otley Chevin and the more laid-back Rombalds Moor.*

This solid, direct march is traced until a sharp turn for the farm, where keep straight on a part-kerbed way by the fence. Over to the right is the bank of Haddockstones Plantation, which has grown around a group of old delphs. *Stone quarried here was a gift from the Farnley Hall estate for the building of Newall workhouse at Otley, now part of Wharfedale General Hospital. Looking back, mile upon mile of the Wharfe Valley is on parade, down to Arthington Viaduct.* As the track enters the top end of the wood remain on an inviting grassy way outside the wall, maintaining this gently ascending line along an extended, well-defined bank top. A TV mast appears ahead, and with a sunken green way dropping to a farm, take a small iron gate on the right. Rise away with a wall, and halfway up take a stile on the right into a field corner. Rise away with the wall to your left, and approaching the brow angle gently away, aiming for the right edge of Crag Plantation ahead.

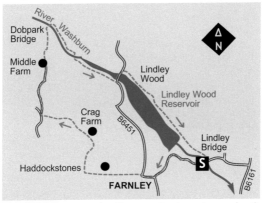

From a bridle-gate under the wood edge, descend a fieldside to a gate onto a farm road in front of the house at Crag Farm. Go left on the walled cart track above the buildings, rising gently away beneath the wood to a gate out into a field. Simply remain on this improving track as the wood ends. It continues gently rising past a range of disintegrating walls before levelling out. *Great views soon look over bracken slopes down into the valley, featuring Lindley Wood Reservoir.* Forge delightfully on until at the end the track turns left, through a gateway with a 'F' inscribed boundary stone at its base. Advance on through gorse to a moist corner with makeshift stepping-stones. From the corner gate a walled, grassy way rises onto the traffic-free, cul-de-sac road to Dob Park. Turn right, descending with excellent views over the Washburn Valley.

Further down, the road winds down a steep wooded bank prior to its demise at Middle Farm. *Note the old house with mullioned windows set back in the yard.* A rough lane takes over to snake down to the valley floor, and brings arrival at Dobpark Bridge. *This celebrated old bridge gracefully arches the wooded Washburn, matched by stone setts running down to a ford: it is the unofficial emblem of Washburn country.* Leave the old road climbing the bank, and from a stile on the right a path runs downstream through leafy Norwood Bottom, immediately joining a broader pathway. *While not in intimate contact with the river, it affords good views over it to a wider landscape.* After crossing an open meadow where the path follows the left-hand wall rather than the river, the way is taken across the river's tree-lined course on a water company bridge. The path resumes downstream to the head of Lindley Wood Reservoir, winding through verdant surrounds to a stile/gate onto the B6451.

Across the embankment bridge turn right through a gateway beneath a house on the opposite bank. The path quickly broadens into a carriageway plunging into trees to run close to the reservoir. *Constructed by Leeds Corporation in 1875, it covers some 117 acres.* The entire way is unexpectedly non-claustrophobic to reach the large grassy dam alongside its concrete outflow. A narrower path forges on to return to the trees, broadening to rise and run along by an old millpond to emerge alongside a lodge onto Cinder Lane just above Lindley Bridge.

Dobpark Bridge

WASHBURN LAKES

A simple circuit of twin lakes, easily split in two if desired

START *Fewston (SE 186537; LS21 2NP)*

DISTANCE *6^{1}4 miles (10km)*

ORDNANCE SURVEY 1:25,000 MAP
Explorer 297 - Lower Wharfedale & Washburn Valley

ACCESS *Start from Yorkshire Water's Swinsty Moor car park on North Lane above Fewston dam. Permissive paths.*

Swinsty Moor car park is a popular starting point for walks around both Swinsty and Fewston reservoirs, and also features WCs, a fishing office, and often an ice cream van. Nearby, across the dam just off-route, is Fewston church. It is difficult now to imagine Fewston as the community it was before the reservoirs came: a tiny Post office survived into the 1990s. From the car park take a broad, firm path heading away to the right behind the WCs. This runs through trees to soon reach a cross-paths. Here take the thinner but still firm one slanting down to the left to quickly alight onto a rough access road just above Swinsty Reservoir.

Turn right to the end of the dam, passing beneath Swinsty Hall en route. *This secluded house dates from 1570, its gabled facade featuring a three-storeyed porch and an arrangement of mullioned and transomed windows.* Cross the Swinsty Embankment with its great views down the valley. At Swinsty Cottage (the old keeper's house) follow the water company road out to a gateway at the end of Pinfold Lane. *En route you pass an ornate valve house concealing a brass plaque recording the opening of the reservoir by Leeds Corporation Waterworks. Some 200 yards further along Pinfold Lane are the remains of the pinfold itself, where stray farm stock was kept. If taking a look, then you could continue to the through road at the end and turn down to rejoin the main route.*

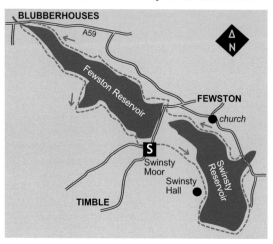

From the gateway the main route takes a firm path on the left, running between the shore and Swinsty Woods to soon emerge onto a road. Go left along the embankment with attractive Swinsty Lagoon on the right. Immediately across, turn left beneath Stack Point car park, and another firm path makes an enjoyable walk along Swinsty's eastern shore. *Part way on, a sign sends a path up through trees to the Washburn Heritage Centre with tearoom, set within the church grounds. It is open weekends/Bank Holidays, April-October and Sundays/Bank Holidays, November to March. St Lawrence's church boasts a solid 14th century tower. The rest was rebuilt in 1697 after a fire, making it a rare, outstanding example of church architecture of that period: note the original thatched roofline of the old nave on the tower wall. Amongst the gravestones the best known bears a 30th February date.*

In springtime a fine array of bluebells is ranged beneath the many native trees on your right. The shoreline walk ends with a climb up the eastern end of Fewston Embankment, with a branch path slanting up through trees just a little earlier. These merge at a gateway onto the road, with Fewston Cottage (another former keeper's house) on the left. *Most of the reservoir is on view here, largely surrounded by trees as is the glimpse of Swinsty Reservoir downstream. Both were constructed in the 1870s, each covering 153 acres and holding 850 million gallons. For a rapid finish, turn left over the embankment on a roadside footway.*

Cross straight over the road and up a stepped path into trees. Turn left on a path at the top - not as per map, despite having been like this for many years. The broad path runs a short way through trees before a gentle drop to the shore. *This earns a massive open view, its wilder feel enhanced by a moorland skyline high above sheep pastures on the other bank.* This firm path leads unfailingly all the way along the northern shore beneath dense plantations. Towards the head of the lake the path curves around beneath the now parallel A59 - again not as per map, but in existence for many years. The path emerges onto a roadside footway to turn the two minutes left over the River Washburn to reach Blubberhouses car park.

Blubberhouses boasts a name of some jollity, and a reputation for providing the district's first snow-blocked road of the winter. This scattered community sits astride the busy Skipton to Harrogate road. St Andrew's church would have seen its fullest congregations during reservoir construction: Fewston's waters lap right up to the road. The Hopper Lane pub is a half-mile up the steep climb towards Harrogate, and a cafe/smokehouse is up Hardisty Hill towards Thruscross.

The return path begins at the end of the car park. This is largely a more pleasant walk, the first stage offering more open views both over the reservoir, and the pastures on your right. A sizeable arm on this side begins at a nice wooded knoll with little paths and seats. The path makes a loop around to bridge inflowing Thackray Beck, and soon returns to the main body of the lake. The last stage is a short one: with the dam approaching, a major fork at a little bay sees the right-hand path rise briefly through trees to emerge directly opposite the car park.

TIMBLE LANDSCAPES

Delightful rambling in the heart of the Washburn Valley

START *Timble (SE 179529; LS21 2NN)*

DISTANCE *5¹4 miles (8¹2km)*

ORDNANCE SURVEY 1:25,000 MAP
Explorer 297 - Lower Wharfedale & Washburn Valley

ACCESS *Start from the village centre, roadside parking.*

Timble is a tiny village on a broad ridge descending from the moors to the Washburn Valley. Its homely inn, a long-time ramblers' favourite, was resurrected in a new guise in 2009 after several closed years. Across the street is the Robinson Gill Library and Free School, the gift in 1891 of a local lad who found fortune in America. Along the street is a Methodist chapel of 1835. From the phonebox take the byway left of the pub to join and go left on a back road. *Immediately glorious views look down the Washburn Valley.* Leaving the houses, look for a narrow enclosed footway on the right after Highfield Farm. Initially overgrown and sometimes muddy, it offers an unfailing descent to a confluence at Timble Gill Beck. Across, the path heads away within the confines of a tiny sidestream: ignore a gate on the right and the path rapidly escapes to run parallel. Before long the path runs left to a gate out into a field. *Big views look over the dale to Sword Point, while Snowden Crags rise closer on the moorland of Snowden Carr just ahead.*

Advance straight on with an old wall, which fades but points to a broad, enclosed green way ahead. After a bend this resumes your course, an obvious line running on to pass above bluebell-floored Holt Wood. From the left-hand of two adjacent gateways a track continues along a field top to become enclosed again, on above Manor House to join its drive. This leads out onto narrow Snowden Carr Road at lovely Low Hall. Advance on a short way beneath the open country of Snowden Carr, and 50 yards beyond Sandhill Farm's drive take a stile on the left. *Swinsty Reservoir now appears back to the left beneath the Menwith Hill radomes, with Lindley Wood Reservoir down-dale.*

Slant right to a wall-stile and maintain the slant to a ladder-stile just above Carr Farm. Cross straight over the drive and on to a corner stile, and on the next field bottom to a stone slab and corner stile. *Rising above the trees straight ahead is the ruin of Dobpark Lodge, a 17th century hunting lodge from the ancient Forest of Knaresborough.* Cross again to a gateway onto an old green way that served the ruined farmhouse just below.

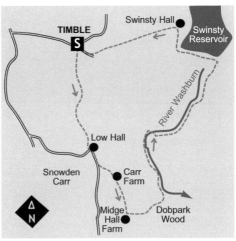

Cross to a stile/gate opposite from where an enclosed way runs on to bridge tiny Snowden Beck, then rises away to a grassy fork beneath Midge Hall Farm. Take the left branch which runs a lovely course to a small gate into Dobpark Wood. It descends near the left edge through increasing carpets of springtime bluebells. Ignoring any branches, towards the bottom it forks: take the right branch over a streamlet to run on to a wall at the wood edge above Snowden Beck's steeper confines. Through a couple of stiles you emerge into a lower section of woodland. *Its springtime carpet of bluebells is mind-blowing.* The path drops down to a gateway in the bottom corner, and forks: go left, dropping to a small metal gate by Snowden Beck. Go right a few yards then cross it, the path bearing right through trees to a gateway alongside the River Washburn. Follow this pleasantly upstream through a couple of sheep pastures. In the third a path forms to rise up a small bank, slanting back down the short way to a footbridge on inflowing Timble Gill Beck. *This replaced the Adamson Memorial Bridge, a miniature packhorse bridge of 1966 that succumbed to floods after a deluge in June 2009.*

Across, ignore a stile accessing the stepping-stones of Rakebridge Hippings on the river, and resume upstream by gorse the short way to a stile before a farm bridge on the river. Across this, turn left on a track upstream. At a gate this swings uphill, leaving a better path clinging to the tree-lined riverbank. Entering a flat pasture with the grassy dam of Swinsty Reservoir just ahead now, cross the centre to a wall-stile ahead. A splendid grassy path rises right, passing a wall corner to run between gorse and pines out to a gate onto an access road alongside Swinsty Cottage (the old keeper's house). *Swinsty Reservoir was constructed in the 1870s, covering 153 acres and holding around 850 million gallons: it appears totally surrounded by woodland.*

Cross the embankment and take a stile in front. A stepped path climbs alongside trees to turn right, passing through a stile into woodland. At once take a gap in the adjacent wall and bear right on the broad path, soon reaching another old wall slanting left. This quickly leads to a gap on the left, from where the path slants gently up to a path junction outside a wall enclosing Swinsty Hall. *Just visible below, this secluded, imposing house dates from 1570, its gabled facade featuring a three-storeyed porch and a fine arrangement of mullioned and transomed windows.* At the junction turn left up a broad path through the trees, soon reaching the top of the wood. Through adjacent gates/stiles ascend the field centre to a corner gate/stile. Resume up the hedgeside to another, then veer gently left to a gate midway along a wall ahead, with a dewpond to the left. Advance up another field to a gate/stile onto the end of a walled, grassy way that rises delightfully back to Timble. Joining an access road, conclude up this, absorbing your outward route.

HANGING MOOR

Moorland and riverbank walking amid unsung countryside

START *Blubberhouses (SE 168553; HG3 1SU)*

DISTANCE *$5^3$4 miles ($9^1$4km)*

ORDNANCE SURVEY 1:25,000 MAP
Explorer 297 - Lower Wharfedale & Washburn Valley

ACCESS *Start from Yorkshire Water's Blubberhouses car park on A59 at head of Fewston Reservoir. Skipton-Harrogate bus.*

Blubberhouses is known largely for its location astride the busy Skipton to Harrogate road, though the Hopper Lane pub a half-mile up the steep climb towards Harrogate regularly waylays travellers. This scattered community also extends up Hardisty Hill featuring a smokehouse with cafe, while St Andrew's church sits south of the main road. It would have seen full congregations during construction of the reservoirs: Fewston's waters lap right up to the main road.

Cross the main road and just to the right a flight of steps descends to the River Washburn. An excellent permissive path heads upstream, remaining with the river for a considerable time. After the idyllically sited cricket club and a rocky scar on a bend you have open fields alongside. Across them is the lengthy distinct line of a tree-lined mill goit. Entering woodland the path runs alongside the extensive old millpond of Low Dam to a path junction at a wall incorporating a seat. *Boulder-strewn Limekiln Plantation is being restored to the native*

57

oak woodland it was long ago. A little further you emerge into a clearing and cross the river at a ford/footbridge. *Up-dale is a glimpse of the massive concrete dam of Thruscross Reservoir.* A broader path slants the short way up onto a firmer access track. Go left a few strides then double back right along a level access road beneath a plantation. This ends at a gate beneath the dam, and a part-stepped path ascends the wood edge onto a road at the dam's western end.

Thruscross is the highest and youngest of the Washburn Valley's four lakes, constructed as recently as 1966. Cross the dam and the road swings left past the old keeper's house. Just beyond, a firm path breaks off left to run parallel through trees. After a few minutes it swings left away from the road: here take a much thinner path right, rising very gently through scrub to a T-junction. Go right on the path running a few yards to a stile back onto the road as its starts to climb towards the Stone House Inn.

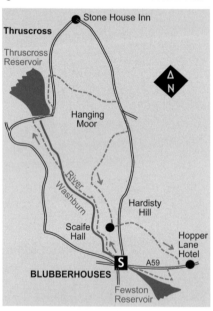

Cross straight over to a gate from where an inviting grassy track heads away between walls set back. *Immediate views look back over the reservoir.* Rising gently to a gate into the open country of Hanging Moor, a thinner path takes over with the fence on the right. As the fence quickly swings right the path swings left, commencing a splendid slant up through heather, featuring a lengthy section of stone causey. *This is a superb example of an old packhorse route linking the Washburn and Nidd Valleys.* Easing out after the flags end the path runs with a ditch, crossing it to continue on to meet a broader grass track. Advance along this to alight onto a firm track, going left the short way to a gate onto Greenhow Hill Road. *As the moor will shortly be rejoined, it is possible to make use of Open Access and trace the wall along to the corner where the main route comes back in.*

Turn right for a few minutes, passing a junction to soon reach the end of the moor. Re-entering at a stile/gate, a faint way runs the short way with a wall to a corner where it fades. Ultimately you will follow the wall to the foot of the moor, but for the next five minutes choose this: faced with mixed terrain, bear right a short way to find a grassy path beneath a bracken slope. Dropping briefly left it ends above a couple of prominent mine spoilheaps just below. Pathless again, drop to your right, aiming to rejoin the wall beneath a second corner and avoiding the worst of a brief boggy section in between. Back at the wall trace its dead-straight course downhill, a thin path forming during a steady descent to a fence-stile in the corner.

Drop down a few strides with a fence onto a broad path at a gate/stile. Go left through this, and a faint grass track crosses a field to a gate at the end. The firmer track runs on beneath a fence to arrive at Scaife Hall Farm. From a gate on the left of the farm, steeply ascend the right side of a fence to a wall-stile back onto Greenhow Hill Road at Hardisty Hill. *Pause to enjoy a retrospective view over the farm to Kex Gill.* Cross straight over and along an access road past a former Methodist chapel to a T-junction at some scattered houses. Turn right to its early terminus at the last house. *Big views look south over the head of Fewston Reservoir.*

From a tiny gate in the corner take a gate in front to follow a walled grassy way, ending at a gate. Advance a little further with the wall, and at a gateway on a minor brow, take a stile on the right. Now follow the wall left along a field top, the wall crumbling as you steer a curious course around to the end. Here you find a wall-stile above a streamlet: advance the short way above the wooded streamlet to a wall-stile at a fence junction. Crossing the streamlet slant left up the field, being ushered right by an old boundary to a stile at a fence/wall junction. Here steps lead down onto a deep wooded hollow of the A59. Turn right on the verge and cross with care, quickly reaching a parking area on an old bend. A stile by a gate sends a good path into Fewston Woods. Quickly forking, bear right down through a gateway onto the firm Fewston Reservoir path. Turn right on this around the head of the reservoir to rejoin the road just short of the car park.

THRUSCROSS RESERVOIR

A reservoir circuit with a splendid moorland sandwich

START Thruscross (SE 153573; HG3 4BB)

DISTANCE 4$\frac{1}{2}$ miles (7$\frac{1}{4}$km)

ORDNANCE SURVEY 1:25,000 MAP
Explorer 297 - Lower Wharfedale & Washburn Valley

ACCESS Start from Yorkshire Water's Thruscross Reservoir car park on Reservoir Road at west edge of dam. Permissive paths.

Thruscross Reservoir is the highest and youngest of the four Washburn lakes, its 120ft high dam constructed as recently as 1966. Sacrificed was the hamlet of West End, which has returned to daylight in times of drought. A mile north of the start is the isolated Stone Cross Inn. Cross the road to find a broad path down through Thruscross Woods to the reservoir. This runs an unbroken course along the bank, soon reaching the submerged West End-Thruscross road: trace it uphill a few strides to a footbridge to resume. Further, the reservoir's western arm passes a ruined mill. *Its waterwheel socket is still evident, and beyond it you trace the course of the leat that supplied it.* The feeder stream of Capelshaw Beck leads out to a stile onto a road. Without joining it the path runs right to a footbridge, then up a verge to turn right through a gate. This new path traces the other side of this western arm beneath Whitmoor Farm, initially looking across at the mill before entering trees.

Part way along, just past the intriguing ruin of Holme Field Head in the adjacent field, you reach a stile on the left. Here leave the concession path and turn right outside the forest fence to a stile/gate onto Whit Moor. A path runs along the fenceside, and part way on merges with another at a guidepost to your left. This runs on to a stile by a gate to drop to a seat on the forest corner, overlooking the valley. A steep path outside the trees drops to a bridge on the River Washburn. *This fine little beck draining the moors is currently unaware of what awaits it in the next few miles!*

Over a stile you stay in open country, beginning with a short ascent to a bouldery knoll at the plantation corner. The path then rises more gently away across Roundell's Allotment. *Beyond the plantations hiding the reservoir, moorland skylines lead from Rocking House to the Great Pock Stones.* Intermittent marker posts see the path across the moor to pass beneath a small boulder cluster on a knoll.

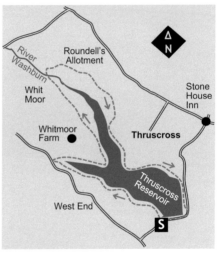

Over a stile/gate you enter heather moorland, a delightful section that ends all too soon. Back among bracken, and with the reservoir re-appearing, a broad grassy path drops right to a ladder-stile at the plantation corner. Steps drop you steeply by the trees to a path running left beneath sheep pastures above the lake.

Further on it drops to the shore, swinging left at a promontory where the dam appears ahead. After an inner corner it re-crosses the old road met earlier, and resumes along the shore until masked by trees. It continues parallel with a road until joining it: turn right past Thruscross Reservoir Lodge to the east end of the dam. Cross the dam road to finish, with steps at the end up into the car park.

JOHN O'GAUNT'S CASTLE

Reservoirs, hamlets, history, forest and rock outcrops

START *Stainburn Moor (SE 236522; HG3 1TQ)*

DISTANCE *7³4 miles (12¹2km)*

ORDNANCE SURVEY 1:25,000 MAP
Explorer 297 - Lower Wharfedale & Washburn Valley

ACCESS *Start from Forestry Commission's Stainburn Moor car park, 2 miles west of B6161 at Beckwithshaw. Permissive path at start.*

Rejoin the road and go right a few minutes to a water company access road left. With grass verges it runs through rank moorland and wooden huts from an old Leeds University research station. *Ahead are the Menwith Hill radomes and Knabs Ridge windfarm.* As the road enters the surrounds of Scargill Reservoir, continue down past the keeper's house. Close by the dam the road drops by a plantation and along the valley floor through colourful woods. Remain on this as it bridges Scargill Beck for the third time, and just beyond crosses the main stream, Oak Beck. *Over to the left are the remains of Beaver Dyke Reservoir's grassy dam, decommissioned in 2013.*

Across the bridge, leave by a stile on the right and ascend the fieldside. Part way up, as a wall takes over, take a gate in it and rise to a gate onto a track junction at Long Liberty Farm. Turn left past some barns, and beyond an old keeper's house the track takes a gate/stile into a field above a plantation. At the far end a gate admits to the wood top and a green way runs on before dropping to a gate out of the trees. *Just beyond is an old gatepost dated 1710.* Just ahead you reach John o'Gaunt's Reservoir: keep straight on beneath a colourful bank outside the reservoir wall. This slants up the bank before resuming to cross a streamlet. From the gate beyond, the path runs on above a seat. *A knoll across the water is occupied by the remains of a hunting lodge from the days of the deer forest, known as John o'Gaunt's Castle. The water tank behind your seat, meanwhile, offers an irresistible choice of Harrogate Corporation's Mild Sulphur Water and Strong Sulphur Water!*

Resuming, the path passes left of a ruin, curving round to drop down a wallside beyond to a kissing-gate. Head away with a fence to your right to rise to a walled green way. Turn left to an early corner, the start of the linear earthwork of Bank Slack. *This gorse-draped bank and ditch was possibly a 5th century defensive boundary, its defined course seen heading away right.*

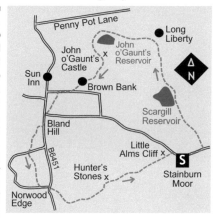

Your route leaves this by passing through the old wall on the left and descending the steep fieldside to a stile at the bottom. This leads to a short embankment above the reservoir head. From a stile at the end, the path slants left up the bank towards the waiting knoll. Part way up, a stile in the fence on the right is your onward route. For now ascend a further minute to the top, passing through a gate to the renovated farm at Haverah Park Top. From here you can appraise John o'Gaunt's Castle. *Within distinctive grassy banks the scant remains are quite impressive in their own atmospheric way, enhanced by the scenic location. An information panel can't be read without entering the private grounds!*

To continue drop back down the path and take the stile on the left, from where a thin path slants up the bank. Rise left by a line of trees, past a low ruin on your right and straight on up, with an old wall and ditch on your right. Pass through a stile in a crumbling wall, with the wooded grounds of East End Manor on your right. Pass through a gateway at the end, then swing right with the wall along the fieldside just outside the grounds. *This lovely old house features mullioned windows and a fine range of outbuildings.* At the end cross a stile/gate onto the drive, across which bear left to a wall-stile opposite. Maintain the direction to a stile just before a gate in the corner, then follow the wall curving round towards the houses at Brown Bank. Through a further stile continue to a gate into the hamlet. *The first house is a former chapel, with an outer stone staircase rising to a porched entrance.*

Pass through a gate and along the front of the buildings. Ignore the access road which swings left, and after a barn at the end, take a gate directly in front. Escape this unkempt corner by tracing the wall on the right, quickly stumbling upon a flight of concrete steps aiding a steep descent. *There are a remarkable 92 in all, along with the remains of an old iron handrail: this would have been the route to chapel for residents of the surrounding Norwood hamlets.*

At the bottom continue with the adjacent wall to a stile in the corner, over which turn left on the enclosed fieldside path to a stile onto Watson's Lane. Turn right on this dead-straight road, passing a house and on to a slight bend. *Ahead are views over the Washburn Valley which you are now entering, featuring Fewston Reservoir.* From a stile by a gate on the left, follow a wall away to a tiny corner gate, and resume on the other side to the next stile. The hamlet of Bland Hill, Norwood, is just ahead. Slant diagonally down the field to a corner stile, from where a splendid embowered green path runs on to emerge between houses onto the road.

Turn right past Norwood Social Hall to the junction by the phonebox, and cross to go left on the ample verge of the B6451. Very shortly after crossing a driveway leave by a stile in the low wall on the right, and head away alongside a wall towards a cluster of houses at Cooper House. Through a gate/stile at the end, bear left straight across the field centre to a gate/stile in the facing wall. *Swinsty Reservoir is seen directly below you.* Continue away along the wallside, through a gateway and then take a tumbledown stile to the right of a gate ahead under a solitary oak tree. This leads to the other side of the wall. From the corner stile just ahead advance with the wall until it turns off, then bear right across this colourful pasture to a wall-stile and slab bridge on a streamlet, a little left of a gate. Ascend the field behind, bearing left to a gate in the far left corner onto narrow Brat Lane.

Turn right a few steps then take a stile on the left. Head away with a colourful hedge, on through an old hedge in the corner and then ascending a fieldside. Continue up to a metal hand-gate in an old wall, and up to a small gate in front of an old house, Cherry Tree Farm. Bear left to a gate and skirt the outside of the grounds, rising to a bridle-gate onto the drive. Ascend this steeply up onto another back road, Top Lane, and turn left to a T-junction with the B6451 again at Norwood Edge. Turn right very briefly then escape left into a parking area at the corner of Norwood Edge Plantation.

Ignore the main track rising away, and take a clear, thinner path diagonally right. This runs a level course before a little pull and shorter gentler drop to a fork. By now broader, take the left branch curving uphill to soon gain another junction. Keep right on the main way, another level course though the trees to a point where an open field abuts the wood on your right. Forge straight on the largely excellent path's level course back into woodland. The wood edge remains very close on your right, and before long a cross-paths is reached at an inner field corner. 150 yards before this point a thinner but clear path rises left the few strides to a couple of boulders, immediately behind which is an old wall and the splendid boulders of Hunter's Stones in a heathery clearing.

Leave by turning right on a clear path that meanders through the outcrops, and immediately shadows the old wall through the trees. Within 150 yards you meet a junction with a short path back to the broad one you left for the boulders. However, simply keep straight on here, clinging to the crumbling wallside path as trees zealously encroach – though the whole way is a dead-straight march beneath a broad break. Eventually the end of the forest comes at a stile in a boggy corner, with the rocky boss of Little Alms Cliff straight ahead. With plantations still to the right, advance on through sheep pasture until approaching the rocks, when a faint path angles left towards the knoll. *This kid brother of Almscliff Crag - three miles distant to the south-east - is also known as Almias Cliff, and is a grand spot to halt.* A clear path heads away to a stile onto a road, with the start point just to the right.

ALMSCLIFF CRAG

Easy walking to a celebrated rocky landmark and viewpoint

START *Huby (SE 275474; LS17 0AJ)*

DISTANCE *6$\frac{1}{2}$ miles (10$\frac{1}{2}$km)*

ORDNANCE SURVEY 1:25,000 MAP
Explorer 297 - Lower Wharfedale & Washburn Valley

ACCESS *Start from crossroads by station. Roadside parking on Weeton Lane. Bus from Harrogate, Leeds, Bradford, and Leeds-Harrogate trains (Weeton station)*

Huby is a commuter village astride the busy A658 Harrogate-Pool road. It has no services other than a railway station, though even this is accorded the name of neighbouring Weeton, almost a mile away. From the station cross the main road to Strait Lane, with an optional pedestrian crossing. Follow this up towards the village edge, and look for signed footpaths going both ways. Take the one on the right, a narrow snicket between houses to quickly pass through a low wall-stile to a fork in front of a field. Take the left branch, remaining enclosed behind gardens to reach Crossfield Cottage. Follow its drive up onto the sloping suburban Crag Lane.

Cross to an enclosed green path rising away, quickly swinging right to run along the backs of gardens into a field. *This good moment earns an impressive prospect of Almscliff Crag rearing majestically above.* Advance on the field edge through a kissing-gate and continue to the far end. From a corner kissing-gate, drop through a wood corner to a tiny stream and kissing-gate behind. A path slants up the sloping field to a fenced wood above. Go briefly right and then left with it to a kissing-gate onto a driveway serving Cragg Hall (Holly Hill on the map). Cross to a stile opposite and a path runs left around the field top to a stile into an old farmyard. Turn right on the track into a field.

Now cross the field bottom to a stile in the hedge opposite, and on through a small scrubby field to a stile and tiny stream amid hollies. Now slant steeply left to a stile in a rising hedge, and maintain this line up across a number of fields, partly aided by white marker posts to reach a wall-stile onto North Rigton's Crag Lane. *Pause to survey a fine panorama back over the Wharfe Valley.* Turn right here, noting, for your return route, a stile by a seat. Past the picturesque New House Farm is a sharp bend at the edge of North Rigton.

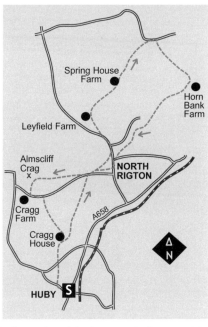

Here turn left up a leafy, enclosed footway, swinging round to a stile sending a good path along the length of a slender, wooded enclosure. At a grassy area at the end, cross to a wall-stile in the left corner. Head out past attractive stone dwellings to a tiny green onto a road at Rigton Hill, opposite the village garden. Turn left, passing a larger green to commence a descent from the village on High Moor Road. When it swings left after a de-restriction sign, advance through a kissing-gate to descend the fieldside. *Ahead is*

the gentle side valley of Nor Beck, while Almscliff Crag re-appears over to the left. In the bottom corner are a stile and footbridge, then resume to join the rising hedge on your right. After a fence-stile towards the top, take a gate on the right and slant up to the top hedge. Part way on, take a stile to resume on its top side. At an early kink use a small gate to put the hedge back on your left. From a squeezer-stile in the corner beyond, Spring House Farm appears ahead. Bear left to a stile under a telegraph pole, then cross a paddock to a corner gate. A track leads down between large barns into the open yard of a riding centre.

Cross to the far right corner to join the access road. Remain on this as it winds out to a junction, keeping right (Rudding Lane) to run out onto a through road at Rudding House. Turn right, and just after the bend take a gate on the right. Through a gate/stile just behind, continue away along a wallside. Just short of the bottom take a gate in the wall to conclude down the other side. In the very bottom a gate and bridge see you back over Nor Beck, from where a path rises left to a bridle-gate. Through this it slants left up a colourful bank, a good place to sit and linger. At the top corner is a bridle-gate and bridleway junction at a wood corner: turn right up the wallside to the brow. Don't advance to Horn Bank Farm just ahead, but take a gate/stile in the wall on your right. Head directly away to a bridle-gate, with Almscliff Crag shining like a distant beacon ahead. *Fine open views are now enjoyed from this broad ridge, with the valley of Nor Beck across to the right and the broader Wharfe Valley over to the left.*

Simply maintain this line all the way, generally with a wall for company as you pass through several bridle-gates, at times fully enclosed. The improving path drops to pass a wildlife pond then transforms into an enclosed leafy footway. Rising gently, when it swings sharp right leave by a wall-stile on the left and resume the direction with a hedge on your right. When this swings away, advance straight on to a stile ahead, and continue through several small fields dropping away to the left. At the end of a longer field is a stile into a fork. Take the clear left branch through an unkempt tract, encountering an early stile: the village is just ahead now. Through a small gate at the very end, advance to a stile to follow a short drive out past attractive cottages onto the road in North Rigton.

Turn left to the junction by the Square & Compass pub. *Village stocks and a war memorial stand on the little green opposite. The modest little church of St John dates from the late 19th century.* Go right past a converted chapel, and as the road starts to drop away, bear right on suburban Brackenwell Lane. Almost at once two paths go off right, either side of a house: take the second of these, a narrow snicket that swings left to run behind gardens, rising steadily to emerge via a stile onto the road where you reached the village edge earlier. Now advance the short way to the stile by the seat, then slant up to a stile in the facing hedge. Across a drive head away with the wall on your right, drawn by the now close-at-hand Almscliff Crag. After two squeezer-stiles rejoin a right-hand wall running to a stile into the crag's environs. A path forms to rise past small old quarries to the rocks, which you can ascend easily from this side to the crest of the major outcrop, High Man. Stop when you get here!

Almscliff Crag is a major Wharfe Valley landmark, prominent in views from all around the district. Sat among neatly packaged fields, it is a hugely popular venue for climbers who may well be providing some entertainment: this rough gritstone offers scores of named routes. The extensive panorama embraces the full girth of Rombalds Moor as well as the lesser-known moors north of Ilkley. A section of wall between the two main bluffs of High Man has a perilous stile in it to descend to the base of these main crags. Immediately below are further outcrops known as Low Man, with a path along their base. Go left here, above or below the crags, to some final boulders in a corner where an enclosed footway descends towards Cragg Farm.

A stile leads onto Crag Lane (again), where turn left down to a small group of houses. After the last one (Cliff House) take a gate on the right, dropping to a stile by a gate just below. Slant across to a stile opposite, then turn down the hedgeside. From a stile in the bottom corner descend a field centre to a gate/stile in the hedge below, and then down another hedgeside to a gate where a firm track forms. This descends outside a plantation to a gate into the grounds of Cragg Hall. Drop down to rejoin the outward route on the driveway, and from here retrace your opening steps back into Huby.

KIRKBY OVERBLOW

Rambling through the fields to a historic hilltop village

START *Pannal (SE 305516; HG3 1EL)*

DISTANCE *6³⁄4 miles (10³⁄4km)*

ORDNANCE SURVEY 1:25,000 MAP
Explorer 289 - Leeds **or**
Explorer 297 - Lower Wharfedale & Washburn Valley

ACCESS *Start from the village centre. Roadside parking, notably Crimple Meadows opposite church. Leeds-Harrogate bus and train.*

Pannal *is an attractive little settlement on Crimple Beck, sandwiched between the expanded modern housing of Burn Bridge and Spacey Houses. Focal point is the church of St Robert of Knaresborough, rebuilt in 1772 but retaining a 15th century tower. Pannal has a Post office/shop, while a once popular roadhouse, the Spacey Houses pub has been demolished in recent years.* From the church follow Main Street to the bridge on Crimple Beck, and ascending as Station Road towards the station, take the first right along narrow Mill Lane. When this ends an enclosed path a few strides to the right continues on past a colourful millpond, then on into woodland alongside Crimple Beck. This runs grandly on through trees, crossing a mill-cut and along the wood edge to enter a little housing complex at an old mill yard at Bridge House. *Fine dwellings occupy this yard of the former Pannal cornmill.*

Advance to a gate ahead, then go immediately left to enter a cricket field. From a stile on the left briefly follow the grassy fenceside track heading away, but shortly bear left to a stile and drain crossing at the far corner. Continue gently up the fieldside to stiles taking you across the Leeds-Harrogate railway. Rise away as before up the hedgeside, through a kissing-gate at the top to ascend a steeper, colourful gorse pasture. *This offers a good view back over Pannal and across to the Crimple Viaduct.* At the top a small old quarry site on Swarth Hill leads to a small gate onto the A61 Harrogate-Leeds road.

To reach the other side it may be safer to go right the short way to the bend to see a little further either way, and even then you might wish to send the fastest across first to observe! Opposite is a drive at Walton Head Farm: don't enter but take a stile just up to the right and head away over the little brow. Slant left down the field to a footbridge and a stile in the

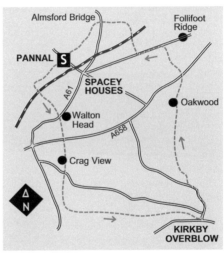

fence opposite, then head away with the hedge on your left. From successive stiles at the end bear right to a hedge-stile to gain access to the A658, Harrogate's 1990s by-pass. With a wary eye on descending traffic in particular, cross to a stile opposite and escape along the field. This same course is maintained to approach a house (Crag View), not quite as per map: after a very brief enclosed section, keep the hedgeside to your right. The way bears left outside the garden wall, and on a short way to a stile into the grounds. Cross the garden to a stile onto the drive going left onto Walton Head Lane.

Again cross straight over to a stile and bear left over this small enclosure to a streamlet and stile, then ascend the fieldside rising away. *By the time the brow is reached you have an excellent view south over the Wharfe Valley to Danefield and Otley Chevin, while Almscliff Crag rises impressively above the fields around Huby.* From a stile on the brow, descend the other side to a corner stile. Cross to another just to the left, then cross a couple of field tops of which the first is enclosed above a horse paddock: new tree plantings are also encountered. From a stile at the end an open field is crossed to a bridle-gate, from where a hedgeside climb of a scrubby pasture leads to a kissing-gate atop the brow.

Resume above the hedge on your right, pleasantly on two lengthy fieldsides above a wooded bank. At the end the tower of Kirkby Overblow's church is revealed just ahead. At the end of a couple of small fields a small gate puts you onto an enclosed path. Pass through the wall-stile on the right to enter a garden. Go left a few strides on the drive and pass through a stile/gate ahead, then bear gently right across a lawned enclosure. A far corner wall-stile puts you into the churchyard, leaving at the far end.

Kirkby Overblow is a hugely interesting village, clustered on an exposed hilltop ridge between the Wharfe and the Nidd. Its name probably derives from 'ore-blower', as iron smelting took place here back in the 13th century. All Saints church was largely rebuilt in 1781, though it retains a 15th century tower. Just 100 yards to its west along the lane is the roadside St Helen's Well at the corner of a house driveway: it is fed by a supply of spring water rising behind it. At one time the village was supplied by around 40 wells. Old Hall and Low Hall are splendid centuries-old houses. Head on past the church to emerge into the village centre. Advance to the junction ahead by the first pub, the Star & Garter, then turn left past the second, the Shoulder of Mutton.

Keep on through the village and out on Follifoot Lane. After starting to climb immediately after Brig Hall (former almshouses), take a stile on the right and ascend with a hedge to the top corner. Over a stile maintain this line (briefly enclosed and then along a triangular fieldside) past a cemetery and to a stile onto a driveway. Across, an enclosed path continues beyond, passing Hill Top Hall and running pleasantly on to emerge into a fieldtop after a couple of sharp bends. *Extensive views look over Spofforth Haggs to the distant Hambleton Hills on the edge of the North York Moors.* A broad, grassy path descends the fieldside to a concrete bridge, then rise gently up a couple of fieldsides. At a corner where the main track rises left, keep straight on the grassy one with the hedge now on your right to lead to a gate in front of Oakwood Farm, now several dwellings. Pass right of the buildings to join the access road heading away to meet Follifoot Lane, this section having been abandoned after its dissection by the by-pass. The driveway turns left to meet the A658 again.

Cross to a bridle-gate opposite at the continuation of the old road. Don't follow it, however, but pass through a bridle-gate on the right and ascend the fieldside path with Pannal golf course just over the wall. At the brow pass through a bridle-gate and on to an enclosed track that drops down onto the Pannal-Follifoot road. Cross and go left on the footway. Ignore two bridleways to the woods and as the road levels out, take a track descending a wall-side on the right at the end of the first field beyond the trees. Part way down it passes to the other side and enjoys a grand stride down to the railway again.

The mighty Crimple Viaduct has by now eased into the view: dating from 1847, its 32 arches carry the Leeds-Harrogate line over the broad Crimple Valley. Cross over the line and continue down a hedgeside to a stile at the bottom, with the bank of Crimple Beck on your right. A little path runs left through some newly planted trees, later passing a pond and running all the way to the end where you rise left to a gate/gap onto the busy A61 at Almsford Bridge.

After one final road crossing turn right on the footway over the bridge, then shortly go left down a short track to a path crossroads in front of a field. Turn left, and an enclosed path heads upstream with Crimple Beck. *Note that a more open option takes the kissing-gate in front, a good path crossing the field to a stile in a hedge, and continuing on near the beckside path to a bridle-gate at the end, where the paths re-unite.* When the beck turns off left the path turns right with a streamlet. Merging with the fieldpath, use the bridle-gate on the left to resume across a field centre. Beyond a stile/gate the broadening way bears right to a stile into the churchyard at Pannal, emerging at the other side onto the road at the start.

OAKDALE & BIRK CRAG

A genteel stroll from the heart of Harrogate,
passing from delightful gardens to woodland crags

START *Harrogate (SE 298553; HG1 2RY)*

DISTANCE *5½ miles (8¾km)*

ORDNANCE SURVEY 1:25,000 MAP
Explorer 297 - Lower Wharfedale & Washburn Valley

ACCESS *Start from the Pump Room in Low Harrogate, just down hill from A61, Parliament Street. Car parks. Bus from Leeds, Ripon, Bradford, Otley; Leeds-Knaresborough-York trains.*

Harrogate is an elegant floral town best known for its spa resort origins: it now thrives as a major visitor and conference centre and cultural resort. Low and High Harrogate developed in early spa days three centuries ago, when people came to take the waters, either by drinking the stuff or finding medicinal value in the baths. High Harrogate is dominated by the 200+ acres of The Stray, an area of open ground left untouched as decreed by George III. Harrogate is the home of the legendary Great Yorkshire Show, which takes place each July: other popular annual events include the International Festival, music festivals, antiques shows, and spring and autumn flower shows. Other permanent features of the town include the Mercer Art Gallery, Montpellier Gardens, Valley Gardens, the Harrogate Theatre and Royal Hall.

The octagonal Royal Pump Room was at the heart of Victorian Harrogate's spa heyday, serving celebrated sulphur water to visitors. It has been preserved as a museum, and the brave can still sample its 'distinctive' taste. From the Pump Room cross the road into Valley Gardens and follow the streamside path to a cafe. *This area is known as Bogs Field, and a notice advises that 36 of Harrogate's 88 mineral wells are found here. The Victorians piped mineral waters to the Royal Bath Hospital and the pump rooms and baths of Low Harrogate. The reverse of the notice sets out in incredible detail the chemical combination of four of the best-known wells.*

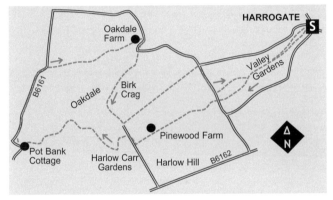

Across the circular garden beyond the cafe, take the main path up the centre of the gardens: this soon reaches a wall corner on the right, just past Magnesia Well Pump Room. *Dating from 1858, this little building has been recently restored within gardens with two well heads behind.* The path resumes up the side of the gardens to ease out at a fork, with a war memorial set back to the right. Leaving tarmac, bear right on the inviting woodland path to the left of the cross. This runs pleasantly on through The Pinewoods to emerge onto Harlow Moor Road. Directly opposite, a tarmac path rises gently back into woodland, soon reaching a large grassy clearing. Pass along the right side of this to head back into trees. The path soon emerges to run along the edge of the woodland, open views to the right emphasized by the presence of a binocuscope. Passing Pinewood Farm it drops onto Crag Lane opposite Harlow Carr Gardens.

These celebrated gardens are run by the Royal Horticultural Society as the North of England's premier botanic gardens. Opened in 1950 to test the suitability of various plants for this northern climate, today they make a hugely popular visitor attraction. The site was first developed as a spa in the 1840s, when a bath-house and hotel were constructed and gardens laid out. Go right 100 yards and turn left down to the former Harrogate Arms. *In its secluded setting, this establishment is the aforementioned 19th century hotel for the adjacent spa, though it has been closed since 2013.*

In the corner below, turn right through a small gate and a path sets off into trees outside the Harlow Carr fence. This runs a smashing course above a stream, fully entering woods and meeting the Harrogate Ringway walk at a fork. Ignore that dropping right to a deep valley bowl with footbridges and keep straight on, just a few strides to another fork where the Ringway goes off left. Again keep straight on the main path keeping right and rising slightly to run an increasingly delightful course through trees alongside an old fence. It drops a little to merge with a path from the right, and on the short way to approach isolated Pot Bank Cottage. At the end the public footpath goes through a kissing-gate in front, passing the cottage to emerge via another gate onto the B6161 Killinghall-Otley road.

Turn right and descend to Pot Bridge, with a stile on the bend sending a short-cut path down the field to a stile at the bottom. Across the bridge climb to the brow, making use of a decent verge for the few minutes along this road. As it rises to a bend with a turnpike milestone just ahead, take a stile at a gate on the right and follow an access track across the field centre to some barns. Keep outside their confines by deflecting left to a corner wall-stile, and head away with the wall on your right. *This spell enjoys big open views over Oakdale and its woods.* The wall turns off at the rocky outcrop of Long Crag: keep straight on down the field, angling gently towards the tree-lined stream on your left. A rough track forms and passes through a gate in an untidy corner. Now enclosed, it runs on the short way to approach Oakdale Farm. As it bends left, take a gate on your right and cross paddocks to a stile/gate and straight on the driveway between exclusive houses. As it swings down to the right after them, go straight on the old road the few strides to Penny Pot Lane.

Cross to the footway and drop right to cross Oakdale Bridge. Entering woods on your right, take the path rising immediately left through trees. Quickly emerging onto a broad level one, turn right. Passing beneath the tumbled boulders of Birk Crag it forks, though they run parallel before rejoining at the start of a steep climb left. Stone steps ascend to the wood top, and then right along the crest of Birk Crag. *Stood atop the crags you can survey wooded Oakdale to rolling fields beyond: definitely the place for a break. These gritstone buttresses are substantial enough to attract rock climbers.*

On your left is isolated Birk Crag House, just after which is a junction, A path remains in the woods with more crags and boulders just below, but you go left the few yards to join the driveway. Go right on this out into the open and on towards Harlow Carr again. Before the gardens however, take an enclosed path left opposite a kennels. This rises to a gentle brow with open views, and maintains a firm course to emerge onto Cornwall Road at a mini-roundabout. Cross and follow the Harlow Moor Road footway right to the start of The Pinewoods. Ignore the first path left and advance a little further to where a path crosses the road. Go left on this through the trees, its good, firm course returning to the war memorial cross. Retrace steps through Valley Gardens, with variations as desired.

At Harlow Carr Gardens

FOLLIFOOT LANDSCAPES

*A ramble to a delightful old village, making use
of what is little short of a historical rail trail*

START *Follifoot (SE 341525; HG3 1DU)*

DISTANCE *6^{1}2 miles (10^{1}2km)*

ORDNANCE SURVEY 1:25,000 MAP
*Explorer 289 - Leeds or
Explorer 297 - Lower Wharfedale & Washburn Valley*

ACCESS *Start from the village centre. Roadside parking.
Harrogate-Wetherby bus.*

Follifoot *is a little village of great character, with a Post
office/shop and the Radcliffe Arms and Harewood Arms pubs. Until
relatively recently the latter was known as the Lascelles Arms, a
change that 'kept it in the family': Edwin Lascelles had Harewood
House built in 1759, and became the 1st Earl of Harewood in 1812
(see WALK 10). Old stocks survive on the side of the green, which
bears a cross with Saxon origins. The imposing Rudding Gates front
an old driveway to Rudding Park.* From the triangular green facing
the Rudding Gates, turn right on Plompton Road leading to the 19th
century church of St Joseph & St James on the village edge. Your
path takes a stile into the end of the churchyard, though first go a
few steps further to view the old pound. *Restored in 1975, this
circular structure would have served to house stray livestock.*

A stile at the bottom of the churchyard sends you down a hedge-side to a stile onto the A658 Harrogate by-pass. Cross with care to another stile and a short path drops down onto a firm track. *This tract of countryside is part of the Rudding Park estate, a vast chunk of which is now a golf course. The present house dates from the 1820s, and operates as a conference centre and hotel.* Go a couple of paces right then follow the track as it runs alongside a sturdy wall on your left, immediately entering the golf course. Remain with this wall all the way, turning sharp left at a cross-tracks, while further on at another track junction, a grassy path takes over. At the very end a fence-stile puts you onto a driveway at Rudding Dower. Turn right the short way out onto Rudding Lane.

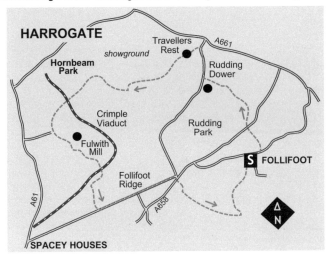

Turn right down Collin's Hill to bridge Crimple Beck, before winding steeply up the other side. Turn off left at the first chance on Crimple Lane, leading to the Travellers Rest. *This is a country pub on the edge of Harrogate, with the county showground just behind it.* A continuing rough lane leads to exclusive residences at Crimple Farm at the end. Advance straight on to a gateway, and briefly through trees to a stile into a sheep pasture. A broad path crosses to a stile/gate into woodland at the end. The two paths heading away quickly merge just before reaching the tall arches of Crimple Valley Viaduct just ahead. The path runs on beneath the nearest arch and down to a concrete track. *The viaduct's ten arches carried the long abandoned Leeds Northern Railway's deviation line off the main route into Harrogate. Omitting the town centre, it looped northwards to Starbeck then on towards Ripon and Northallerton: passenger services ceased in 1967.*

Go left on the concrete track along Crimple Valley floor, but when it turns right keep straight on a path to the beckside on your left, and pass through a kissing-gate to join its bank. The left-most path runs the short way to a footbridge on a sidestream, and a few strides further to a T-junction at the wood edge. *Ahead is Crimple Viaduct of 1847 on the Leeds-Harrogate line.* Turn right on the broad path along the wood edge, rising steadily until the field on the left ends. Here the broadening path slants up to the left to leave the wood at a gate/stile. Joining a surfaced way turn left, quickly merging into a rough access road just short of reaching a road at Hornbeam Park. Go very briefly left on the road to a private gateway, then turn right on the enclosed path into trees. This bridges the railway, and at the end an access road is joined. This swings left and leads behind suburban gardens to meet Fulwith Mill Lane.

Turn left down between the last houses, arriving at the bottom alongside renovated Fulwith Mill Farm with Crimple Viaduct rising behind again. A little lower is the old mill itself, but your track is through a gate straight ahead. Swinging right through another gate, your improved track emerges into a field and quickly swings left with the fence to drop to a farm bridge on Crimple Beck. Bearing left up the other side to a gate, don't pass through but turn right up a hedgeside path. At a bridle-gate at the top you re-cross the former railway you met at Crimple Valley Viaduct.

Resume up a field centre to a bridle-gate accessing a sturdy bridge over the surviving railway. *A 'Panel Loop' sign on the bridge fails to deal with the spelling of nearby Pannal! The line itself runs in a deep cutting to the left, just prior to its 100° curve to cross the great viaduct, still in view.* A cart track turns right, briefly enclosed before emerging into a field. Remain on this splendid path bearing left beneath bracken slopes, and with new plantings on the right. Reaching a gate into a woodland corner, a path rises left through the trees of Spacey Houses Whin alongside an old wall.

Remain on this all the way to the top, emerging from the wood edge for the final strides up onto the Pannal-Follifoot road.

Go left on the footway, gently rising to a brow at Follifoot Ridge. *Visible on the left in the grounds of Follifoot Hall is an old windmill.* Dropping gently down, ignore Haggs Road going off right, and with good verges advance past a riding centre and a business park. Just a little further, a gate on the right sends an enclosed track down to an underpass beneath the A658. Emerging, turn right on a broad bridle-path, which quickly swings left to run a pleasant enclosed course to a sharp bend. *Parallel on your left here is the former Church Fenton & Harrogate branch line: closed in 1964, the section south of Spofforth is now a leisure trail.* When the bridle-way goes right, pass through the kissing-gate in front and head away.

A firm path remains underfoot, broadening into a cart track along the deep trench of the rail cutting. Go straight over an early cross-track and resume for some time amid flourishing vegetation between wooded banks. Further on at a minor clearing, leave by a firm path slanting left up to a kissing-gate, then double back left on an inviting fieldside path. Bear right at the end, briefly on a cart track, then left through a broad gap. The path descends the field-side, swinging right at the bottom and becoming enclosed as it crosses tiny Horse Pond Beck. Remain on this splendid hedgerowed way of Tofts Lane as it runs towards the village. At the head of a suburban street, remain on the track rising left past gardens before turning right to become a firm access lane at houses. Advance briefly on, then as it swings right you might opt for a wall-stile on the left. This path turns right on a tightly enclosed course between gardens, twice swinging sharp left, then right at a junction to emerge via a stile onto the main street.

Rudding Gates, Follifoot

KNARESBOROUGH

A craggy valley explored from a fascinating historic town

START *Knaresborough (SE 350570; HG5 8AL)*

DISTANCE *6³4 miles (10³4km)*

ORDNANCE SURVEY 1:25,000 MAP
Explorer 289 - Leeds

ACCESS *Start from the Market Place. Car parks. Buses
from surrounding towns; Leeds-Harrogate-York trains.*

Knaresborough is a market town with bags of character, perched
on the north bank of a large bend of the Nidd. Overlooking the
deep river gorge are the ruins of Knaresborough Castle. Dating
from the 12th century, it was extended by King John as a base for
hunting in the Forest of Knaresborough. What survives today is
largely the 14th century work of Edward I and Edward II. In the same
century John of Gaunt, 1st Duke of Lancaster, took possession, and
to this day it remains in the hands of the Duchy. In 1644 the town
underwent a six-month Parliamentary siege, during which time the
castle suffered badly. An Elizabethan courthouse survives as a
museum, and the castle grounds form a public park around the
slighted tower. A vibrant market square features pubs, cafes, shops
and the famous old chemist's shop, a pharmacy since 1720. A
market charter was granted in 1310, and markets are still held on
Wednesdays. St John's church features the impressive Slingsby tombs.

An imposing railway viaduct of 1851 straddles the river, with its boating and refreshments. At Mother Shipton's Cave on the far bank you can discover the secrets of this 15th century prophetess, and witness countless articles turned to stone by waters from the Dropping Well. The craggy walls (Magnesian limestone overlying sandstone) overlooking the river secrete other intriguing features, notably the House in the Rocks and the Chapel in the Crag: these feature during the walk. Another local character was John Metcalf, better known as Blind Jack: born in 1717 he was blinded by small-pox at the age of 6, but nevertheless he engaged in a variety of colourful exploits culminating in his better-known road-building achievements. He died at the age of 93, and is buried at Spofforth.

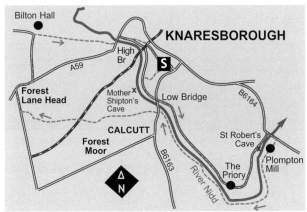

From the cross in the Market Place, head away past the old town hall on your left, and turn left. Keep straight on between the police station and the Castle Inn to quickly enter the castle grounds. Beyond the keep you reach a classic viewpoint overlooking the River Nidd and the railway viaduct. Take the last path on the right near the war memorial, making a steep, partly stepped descent to the riverside attractions on Waterside. Turn left on the road and follow it left past assorted buildings - including the former Castle Mills - to emerge onto the B6163 alongside Low Bridge.

Across the road resume on Abbey Road past the Half Moon pub. Tall cliffs to your left feature the House in the Rocks. *This intriguing* 'house' of 1791 comprises four vertically set rooms: castellations added later saw it become known as Fort Montague. Immediately past it is the Chapel in the Crag. *Its entrance guarded by a carved figure of a knight, this wayside shrine of Our Lady of the Crag dates from 1408, and is normally open on Summer Sundays.* Resume along the quiet road, soon between impressively tall cliffs and the river. A traffic impasse is reached at splendid sandstone houses. *Here in the 13th century a group of friars began work on a priory, thought to be on the site of a chapel that became the resting place of St Robert.* Further, the road reaches modern housing. A small gate on the right marks the entrance to St Robert's Cave, hidden away a few steps down into the trees, overlooking the river.

St Robert of Knaresborough lived a hermit's existence here for almost forty years until his death in 1218. Said to have worked countless miracles, this devout man's quest for solitude became thwarted as he was sought out by pilgrims seeking both physical and spiritual uplift. Before his death he was visited by King John. The cave hewn from the cliff was his original chapel, where a shelf served as an altar. The succeeding chapel built outside is evident in the base of the altar, along with Robert's original grave prior to his removal to the nearby priory.

The road joins the B6164 Wetherby Road on the edge of town. Turn right over Grimbald Bridge then upstream on the other bank. An old drive runs to a popular open area between Plompton Mill Farm and Plompton Mill itself, beneath a caravan site. *This old cornmill is now a café alongside the weir.* Advance along past the last of the caravans where a footpath squeezes up the wooded bank onto a splendid knoll beneath the sandstone face of Grimbald Crag. *From here look down on another weir supplying the former Abbey Mill on the opposite bank, with a waterwheel in place.*

The path drops to the edge of the caravan site, but within a few steps bears right to run above the wooded bank. Dropping back to the river, it traces the Nidd through woodland. After passing a massive house opposite, you emerge into a field. The fenced path crosses it well above the river to reach a drive. Ignore its climb to the left, and keep straight on past a couple of houses, as a path squeezes beneath a massive limekiln. Back onto the riverbank the path resumes beneath steep woodland. A short pull towards the bank top precedes a drop back down to a garden wall, and on to emerge by an interesting house. Follow this lane, Spitalcroft, past other houses out onto the B6163. *Just to the right is the Mother Shipton Inn at Low Bridge, and an optional early finish.*

Cross and turn left up the footway the short way to the end of the houses, above which an enclosed path doubles back right above them. This curves up to emerge via a stile into a field, a rapid escape into open countryside. Rise away with a straggling hedge to your left, at the top curving right to locate an old stile at a kink, with a small pond just to the right. Resume up the hedgeside to a corner stile, and continue away with a hedge on your right. Not all these hedges appear on the map! At the end is a gap between two hedge corners: bear right, with a hedge on your right the path rises gently to a kissing-gate onto the railway line. Cross with care and the path runs left along the edge of Harrogate golf course.

Largely screened by trees, the firm path runs on outside housing to become enclosed before joining a cart track. Go left on this between gardens to emerge onto Forest Lane. Turn right on the suburban footway to meet the A59 at Forest Lane Head. *Diagonally opposite stands a former 18th century tollhouse.* Go right a few yards to cross at the pedestrian lights, and take the footway right to a junction with Bilton Hall Drive. Go left on this around to a junction by the hall entrance, with just a glimpse of the red-brick hall. *Though largely 19th century, parts date back to 1380 when it originated as a hunting lodge: it is currently a nursing home.*

Turn sharp right on an enclosed, tarmac path. *This popular cycle route commemorates local girl Beryl Burton, seven times world cycling champion.* This will lead all the way back, dropping gently through fields to emerge at a path junction at an open area. Take the footpath straight ahead, keeping right at an early fork dropping through trees to rejoin the cycleway just by the river. A short way further it emerges onto the A59 at High Bridge, across which is the main entrance to Mother Shipton's Cave. Cross the bridge and turn right along Waterside past the Worlds End pub. *This recalls one of Mother Shipton's prophecies, which predicts doom should the bridge collapse three times.... and it's already happened twice!* Within a minute or so, turn left up Water Bag Bank, part cobbled past a thatched cottage. Use the rail underpass at the Mitre pub at the station to continue up Kirkgate into town, turning left at the very end to re-enter the Market Place.

NIDD GORGE

First-rate wooded river scenery upstream of Knaresborough

START *Scotton (SE 330584; HG5 9HG)*

DISTANCE *6$\frac{1}{2}$ miles (10$\frac{1}{2}$km)*

ORDNANCE SURVEY 1:25,000 MAP
Explorer 289 - Leeds **or**
Explorer 297 - Lower Wharfedale & Washburn Valley

ACCESS *Start from the Woodland Trust's Nidd Gorge car park on B6165 on south edge of village. Bus from Knaresborough.*

Scotton is a pleasant village to the north of the Nidd Gorge, featuring the Guy Fawkes Inn and the church of St Thomas. The Nidd Gorge is in the care of the Woodland Trust, and has become *a goood location to spot otters.* From the car park a forest road slants down into the woods, doubling back at the bottom to rapidly arrive at Burgess Bridge over the River Nidd. *Opened in 1988, you shall return to this long, tall footbridge later in the walk.* Cross and turn right on the path upstream, a splendid stroll by the river through Bilton Banks, with various sections reinforced by boards amid springtime bluebells. A brief spell well above its winding bank soon drops back down, with even a little spell by sandy beaches as you leave and then re-enter Woodland Trust land. Remaining hard by the river, an open, scrubby section is met before a sustained spell almost draws level with Scotton Mill on the opposite bank.

Just before this point, an old way (the second of two within a minute) descends to the riverbank, serving an old ford. Turn up its hollowed course, now with wooden steps, to a level path junction: bear briefly right to another junction just around the corner, and take the right branch slanting steadily back to the river at a weir. *This served the converted former Scotton flax mill, which dates from 1798.* Resume upstream just a short way further as far as a sidestream. From the main bridge take the path rising left away from the river, keeping right at a very early fork to emerge into a big field corner. Take the path bearing right, following the wood edge to meet an old railway line alongside the Nidd Viaduct. *Its 100ft tall arches were completed in 1848, carrying the old line to Ripon and points further north over the Nidd Gorge: it closed in 1967, and its parapet offers a good view of the river upstream.*

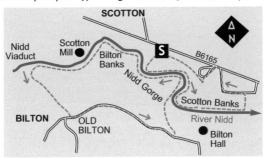

Turn left on the surfaced path on the old railway line, passing sculptures of two local characters and a 'Child of the Future' to reach modern housing at Bilton on the edge of Harrogate. *A plaque marks the site of a narrow-gauge railway that branched off here between 1907 and 1956 to carry coal to Harrogate Gasworks.* Eschew civilisation and turn left on Bilton Lane's quiet footway, almost at once reaching the Gardeners Arms at Old Bilton. *If it's open, step inside to appreciate an array of cosy rooms supplied from a serving hatch.*

Continue along the road, which swings up and around past a caravan site to enter more open surroundings. Passing through a padlocked gate followed by scattered dwellings, leave by a gate on the left at the end of a field after a small cluster of houses. An enclosed track runs the short way to a stile/gate back into Trust woodland. Follow the track running left along the top of the wood, and when it passes through a locked gate instead take the broad path right, remaining outside a fence on your left. Ultimately, at a waymarked fork, take the right branch slanting grandly down the part open bank to the foot of the wood, with the Nidd waiting below.

At the bottom turn upstream through splendid surrounds with craggy walls opposite. This riverside path leads quite quickly back to the footbridge. Re-cross and turn downstream on an excellent riverside path through Scotton Banks. Before long it climbs a steep flight of wooden steps onto the forest road on which you began the walk. Turn right briefly to a corner and take a path back down intermittent steps to the river. Resume downstream on another delectable section to the boundary of the Trust's land, meeting the terminus of the forest road further on.

Continue downstream, an equally beautiful stroll along the foot of unmanaged gardens. In time you arrive at a fenced impasse, and the path turns sharp left to finally leave the Nidd. It climbs between gardens to emerge into the affluent surroundings of Lands Lane. Turn left, then swinging sharp right as Netheredge Drive to rise to the B6165. Go briefly left to a surfaced path going left onto the suburban street of Appleby Crescent. Go left, and bear left again on cul-de-sac Appleby Court. Keep straight on a surfaced path leading out to a play area back on the edge of the woods.

Take the still surfaced path running right outside the houses, and as it prepares to re-enter suburbia, take the regular path bearing left to remain in the trees. This drops onto another path, where go right to continue outside gardens on the wood top, quickly arriving at a sharp corner. *On your left is the grassy knoll of Gates Hill Camp, part of an Iron Age defensive site.* Ignore a path dropping into the wood as the path swings right a short way to an information board. Again ignore a path doubling back left and remain on the wood edge. *During this stage a very distinct bank and ditch run to your left, part of the aforementioned earthwork.* Before long a signed path slants left, over a cross-paths and then contouring around the slope. Merging into a broader path from the right, go left on this above a particularly steep slope and parallel with the nearby road to return to the start.

SPOFFORTH PINNACLES

A beckside ramble leads to fascinating rock formations

START *Spofforth (SE 362510; HG3 1AP)*

DISTANCE $5^3/_4$ *miles* $(9^1/_4km)$

ORDNANCE SURVEY 1:25,000 MAP
Explorer 289 - Leeds

ACCESS *Start from the village centre. Roadside parking on Castle Street, including lay-bys. Harrogate-Wetherby bus.*

Spofforth is an attractive village dominated by its castle ruins dating from the 13th century: home of the Percys since Norman times, their departure to build Alnwick Castle in Northumberland in the early 14th century left Spofforth to decay. There are two pubs, the Railway and the Castle, and a Post office/shop. All Saints church has a 15th century tower and a 14th century monument to Sir Robert de Plompton. John Metcalf, otherwise Blind Jack of Knaresborough (see page 83), was buried here in 1810. Spofforth lost its railway when the Harrogate-Wetherby line closed in 1964.

Leave the road through the village by unsigned Church Lane opposite the shop. This runs past a triangular green and swings right past a mounting block and the church onto the A661. Go very briefly left on a footway as far as Spofforth Bridge on Crimple Beck. Across, turn left upstream, on a path largely adhering to the flood embankment and somewhat overgrown in the height of summer.

Stick close to the beck to pass a footbridge past the last building (the old mill), which you will cross to finish the walk.

Resume along the bank and maintain this course all the way, the path now much improved. *Over to the right several massive gritstone sentinels stand island-like in the fields, outliers of Spofforth Pinnacles. Better examples are seen further on, and will become better known on the return.* The path faithfully traces the beck all the way upstream to eventually emerge onto Plompton Road alongside stone-arched Guilders Bridge. Turn right along the road, rising alongside Plompton Corner Woods back onto the A661. Follow the verge briefly left to cross more safely to a gated road heading away. *This section of the B6163 was abandoned when the Harrogate by-pass was completed.*

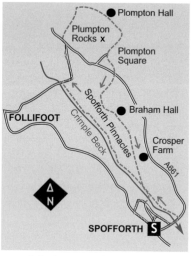

Follow the old road up to a slight brow, with Plompton Hall's stables' octagonal cupola glimpsed across to the right. Fifty yards after a farm drive rises left, turn off right on a track across a large field. At the ends it drops to a dip and a track starts to ascend the other side through trees. Almost at once however, part way up turn right on an unkempt grassy track, rising gently into trees and then curving left as a path through a newly planted area to a bridle-gate. Plompton Hall is now immediately to your left. *The hall was built for Daniel Lascelles around 1760.* With a fence to your left cross the field to a bridle-gate onto the parallel access road, just short of a triangular junction. Turn right on this, leading out above the wooded confines of Plumpton Rocks.

The driveway passes through a pair of lodges at Plompton. Immediately on your right before the lodges, a gate points the way to Plumpton Rocks. *On private land with an entry fee, the grounds are normally open weekends and Bank holidays, March to October. Laid out long ago as pleasure grounds by Daniel Lascelles, this 30-acre park boasts a fine collection of natural gritstone outcrops all interwoven with shrubs, woodland walks and an attractive lake.* Between the lodges, don't descend the road onto the main road, but turn left up the short road to the houses at Plompton Square. Turn sharp right along the first row, continuing at the end on a short enclosed path to a stile out into a colourful pasture. Head away, bearing right to drop to a stile by a gate in the far corner.

Re-cross the A661 to a stile opposite, and a nice little path heads away with the wall outside a wood to a gateway on a gentle brow. This overlooks the Crimple Valley of your outward route, and here you emerge into the splendid environs of Spofforth Pinnacles, a modest version of Brimham Rocks, minus tourists. Bear gently left on a path dropping slightly but remaining near the left edge of the area. You are now looking down on this fascinating collection of randomly sited gritstone monoliths amid the bracken. It runs to the nearest boulder then on beneath two further ones. Through a line of old hawthorns an intermittent path continues to a fence corner outside the sprawling farm at Braham Hall. Pass through a stile to reach a wall corner at the far end of the confines.

Keep on to a minor knoll in front then descend the extensive field, bearing gently right to pass left of an isolated outcrop and left of a small marsh to a fence-stile ahead. Bear right to follow the hedge on the bottom of the enclosure, passing a rectangular pond. Keep on through a gate and beneath further rocks spread amongst successive stiles in the horse paddocks beneath Crosper Farm. Emerging into a lengthy sheep pasture at the end, further massive boulders are still evident nearby as you keep on with the hedge to find a fence-stile halfway along. Over this cross a stone slab bridge and bear left across the arable field to gain the embankment of the outward route. Turn left the short way back to the footbridge, and this time cross it to follow an enclosed path past the old mill. You also cross the deep, dry channel of a former cut on a stone-arched bridge and out onto Mill Lane. *Look back to appraise the substantial three-storeyed former Spofforth Cornmill.* At a junction at the top at the village edge, go a couple of steps left on Clive Road and then either keep left on Church Hill for the church, or turn sharp right on Beech Lane for the castle.

LINTON & SICKLINGHALL

Attractive villages and stately parkland west of Wetherby

START Wetherby (SE 403482; LS22 6NE)

DISTANCE 9 miles (14^{1}2km)

ORDNANCE SURVEY 1:25,000 MAP
Explorer 289 - Leeds

ACCESS Start from the town centre. Car parks.
Bus from Leeds, Harrogate, Tadcaster, Knaresborough.

Wetherby is a fine old market town on the north bank of the Wharfe. Its market charter was granted in 1240, and a market takes place on Thursdays. The town has been vastly extended by modern suburbia to the north, a process aided by completion of its early bypass as the Great North Road was deflected east of the town. Though occupied by the Romans and even earlier, Wetherby was probably at its busiest as a major staging post on this old London to Edinburgh route. Placed midway between the two capitals, its main street would have been lined by coaching inns, some of which survive. The old bridge still carries most traffic into town. Focal point is the market place, in which the old town hall stands island-like. At one side of the square is the market hall, containing the Shambles built in 1811 by the Duke of Devonshire as butchers' shops. The parish church of St James dates from 1841. Wetherby is also home to one of Yorkshire's many celebrated racecourses.

From the Town Hall turn left down Market Place to the bridge on the Wharfe. Across, turn immediately right along Lodge Lane. Its footway quickly leads to a car park alongside a leisure centre. Keep right to find an embanked path commencing a splendid walk upstream, around a big loop of the river containing sports fields at flood-prone Wetherby Ings. *On the opposite bank is the Georgian bath-house passed at the end of the walk.* Soon reaching a long metal footbridge, cross and advance to a surfaced path lined by trees ahead. Running left it ends at a wall-stile, through which an embanked path crosses a field to enter a golf course. Keep straight on, through a clump of trees, across a fairway and ahead on a broad green path to quickly reach a stone-arched underpass on converging with the wooded embankment of the old railway (of which more later). Through this go briefly left, then cross the course to the base of a shrubby bank where a short path rises onto Linton Lane.

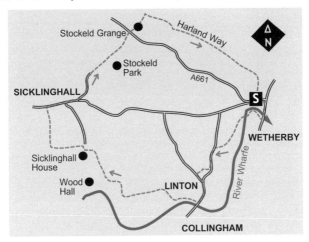

Turn left on the verge path, passing desirable residences into straggling Linton. After a slight drop after The Acres, a tempting grassy branch curves right between gardens to emerge onto the end of an access road, Muddy Lane, which runs out the short way onto Northgate Lane. From the triangular green with canopied pump, go left on the lane back to the through road to reach the historic

Windmill pub. Remain on the footway down to the bridge on the Wharfe. *This was severely damaged by flooding in December 2015, causing closure until September 2017.* Without crossing, turn right on the private road of Linton Common. High above a wooded bank of the Wharfe, remain on this as far as the last of the exclusive houses. Now leave by a steep path ascending the side of a wood, levelling out to run a delightful course through a belt of trees. Emerging onto the surfaced Trip Lane, turn left for a lengthy, level stroll between hedgerows. *This broad ridge boasts fine open views, occasionally left over the valley to Collingham's fringe.*

Further on, alongside Linton Grange gates, the road becomes a private drive to Wood Hall. *Here is a hotel with a Carmelite monastery alongside.* Don't enter but turn right on a broad path through a belt of trees into a massive rolling cornfield. *Big views look up the Wharfe Valley to Otley Chevin and Rombalds Moor.* The path crosses directly to a fence opposite, then bears left to the edge of Lime Kiln Wood. Remain on this path as it turns right through a gateway, tracing the wood edge around two sharp bends before finally entering the trees. Running along the wood top this shaded spell is brief, as the wood corner is reached and the path continues, pleasantly enclosed alongside a tall hedge. Further on it becomes a briefly fully enclosed way, then a grassy cart track forms to lead out onto an access road at Sicklinghall House.

Turn briefly right just as far as the gates on the slight brow where it becomes Longlands Lane. From a bridle-gate on the left a path heads away along the hedgeside. *Over to the right are glimpses of Sicklinghall.* At the end a wood-edge spell is followed by emerging, briefly, before the path turns through a hedge-gap and heads away right, pleasantly broadening, with the village ahead. The track soon becomes enclosed by hedgerows and as Geecroft Lane runs a lovely course along to Back Lane, where drop down the few paces onto the village street, and turn right.

Sicklinghall is an affluent commuter village, featuring the Scotts Arms, a school, village hall, St Peter's church, and a former Wesleyan Chapel of 1822. Also here is the Roman Catholic church of the Immaculate Conception (built in 1848 by the generosity of the Middelton family of Stockeld), and the convent of the Sisters of the Holy Family of Bordeaux. Just beyond the pond, bear left on cul-de-sac Stockeld Lane. This runs down between hedgerows to

Sicklinghall Lodge, continuing as a firm bridleway rising through trees to a gate into Stockeld Park. Almost at once, before the drive swings right, bear off slightly left, passing a tree-shrouded pond in a hollow on your left, and now bearing gently right advance on through archetypal parkland. *Stockeld Park is a splendid stone house completed in 1763 for William Middleton, whose family had owned the manor for more than 450 years. In the 1890s it was acquired by the Foster family of Black Dyke Mills in Bradford, and though still occupied it also opens for various functions.*

At a fence corner with bridle-gate and cattle-grid you join a driveway on your right, following its verge out to a lodge alongside the A661: a bridle-gate is found to the left of the gates. Cross with care and head down the short drive to Stockeld Grange. Drop straight down through the yard and through a gate into the field below. Drop left to a tapering corner, and through the gate an enclosed green way drops down onto an old railway. *With the aid of cycling charity Sustrans, this old line has transformed into a cycle route known as the Harland Way. It traces the bed of the Harrogate-Wetherby railway: originally the York and North Midland Railway's Harrogate branch, it closed in 1964.*

Turn right and remain on this splendid way through greenery back to Wetherby. Initially on an embankment and then through a rock cutting, it later becomes surfaced to run between extensive but unobtrusive housing to reach a major fork at a grassy area. *This is one of the three junctions of Wetherby's rail triangle, where lines to Leeds, Harrogate and Church Fenton met.* Go left, but at the end of the open area take a right fork rising slightly off the old line. This quickly meets a bridleway lane alongside a bridge to your left. Go right on its pleasant course, later dropping past trees and crossing a deep cutting of the third arm of the triangle. Dropping down onto Quarry Hill Lane, this access road runs out onto Crossley Street in the town. With a little cinema to your right cross and go the short way along Caxton Street, then at the end go left on West Gate (the A661) back into the centre. Almost at once on your right you pass the Georgian Baths at Wharfedale Lawns. *A small gate sends a little path down to the splendidly restored 200-year old bath-house, which features a sunken bath fed by spring water. As the fashion had faded, it was sold off by the Duke of Devonshire in 1824.*

INDEX • *Walk number refers*

At Harewood